Lies, Half-Truths, and More Lies

Other books by Herb W. Reich

Don't You Believe It!
Numberpedia
Lies They Teach in School
2,501 Things That Really Piss Me Off
The Odyssey Scientific Library (Editor)
Encyclopedia of Engineering Signs & Symbols (Editor)

Lies, Half-Truths, and More Lies

The Truth Behind 250 "Facts"
You Learned in School (and Elsewhere)

Herb W. Reich

Skyhorse Publishing

Skyhorse Publishing books may be purchased in bulk at special discounts for sales promotion, corporate gifts, fund-raising, or educational purposes. Special editions can also be created to specifications. For details, contact the Special Sales Department, Skyhorse Publishing, 307 West 36th Street, 11th Floor, New York, NY 10018 or info@skyhorsepublishing.com.

Skyhorse® and Skyhorse Publishing® are registered trademarks of Skyhorse Publishing, Inc.®, a Delaware corporation.

Visit our website at www.skyhorsepublishing.com.

10 9 8 7 6 5 4 3 2 1

Library of Congress Cataloging-in-Publication Data is available on file.

Cover design by Rain Saukas

Print ISBN: 978-1-5107-4164-5
Ebook ISBN: 978-1-5107-1605-6

Printed in the United States of America.

Dedicated to all those gullible souls who most need this book.

CONTENTS

Preface   *xiii*

Foreword   *xv*

SECTION ONE: What Can We Believe?   3

A KKK Supreme Court Justice?   5

Underage Congressmen   6

Gunfight at the O. K. Corral   7

The Founding Fathers   8

Noah   10

Sardines   11

First Blood at Pearl Harbor   12

Valley Forge   13

Boycott   14

The Las Vegas Strip   15

Transmutation   16

Missing Days   17

The Border States   18

The Champagne Punt   19

Gandhi   20

Alexander Hamilton Sex Scandal   21

The Tokyo Firebombing   22

Pineapples   23

Quick Ones   24

Dr. Spock Convicted   26

The Virgin Queen   27

Birdman of Alcatraz   28

Jesse Owens's Olympics   29

George Washington's Expense Account   30

Japan Bombs the US   32

Poisoned Booze   33

Mad as a Hatter	34
Statue of Liberty	35
Woman for President	36
Black Thursday	37
Louis Pasteur	38
Marco Polo	39
Conestoga Wagon	40
The Dead Winner	41
Monitor vs. *Merrimack*	42
The White Feather	43
More Quick Ones	44
Lady Godiva	45
King Arthur	46
Sir Thomas Crapper	47
Flamma	48
Aaron Burr's Treason	49
Who Influenced Whom?	50
Hedy Lamaar	51
Unelected President	52
Thanksgiving Dinner	53
Chopin's Minute Waltz	54
Spinach	55
Americans Fighting Russians	56
A Burning River	58
Ending the Civil War	59
The First Novel	60
Franklin Pierce Re-nomination	61
Magna Carta	62
Still More Quick Ones	63
The Revolution's First Casualty	64
The Telephone	65

Contents

G.I.   66

Three Brass Balls   67

Three Volleys Over a Grave   68

Al Capone's Fall   69

Graham Crackers   70

To the Back of the Bus   71

Crucifixion   72

George M. Cohan   73

Blitzed Londoners   74

Pope Gregory and the Black Death   75

Mutiny on the *Bounty*   76

The Croissant   78

The Worst Rigid Airship Disaster   79

The Alamo   80

Plymouth Rock   81

Robbing the Mint   82

Man Versus Beast   83

Yet More Quick Ones   84

Holiday Songs   85

The Kilt   86

Walking Under a Ladder   87

United Nations Location   88

Did Roosevelt Know?   89

Mao's Great Leap Forward   90

Indulging Terrorists   91

Pirate Jean Lafitte Defends New Orleans   92

Roger Williams   93

A Transvestite New York Governor   94

Admiral Farragut Lashed to the Mast   95

Swanee River   96

The Transcontinental Railroad   97

The US Army Versus US Civilians	98
Puritan Christmas	100
Boulder Dam	101
Ferdinand Magellan	102
FDR and the Great Depression	103
John Glenn in Space	104
Disney Banned	105
Again, Quick Ones	106
Martin Luther	107
Mount Vesuvius	108
The NRA	109
Women in Combat	110
Wright Brothers	112
Nero and the Burning of Rome	113
Lightning	114
Traffic Jams	115
Britain's First American Colony	116
Fulton's Steamboat	117
The Flag on Mount Surabachi	118
US Mints	119
The Liberty Bell	120
The IRS	121
Civil War Generals	122
George Washington for President	123
Cowboys	124
The First World War	125
Inventing Champagne	126
The Death of Diana	127
Hamilton and Burr	128
Helen Keller	129
The Chicago Fire	130

Contents

The Light Bulb 132

Other Quick Ones 133

General Patton on D-Day 134

Bombing Civilians 135

Secession 136

Foreign Aid 137

Response to the Gettysburg Address 138

SECTION TWO: Who Says So? 139

SECTION THREE: Experts and Naysayers 153

SECTION FOUR: Politicians 163

Afterthought 177

Preface

This volume is the natural successor to my earlier book, *Lies They Teach in School.*

Soon after that book was published, I realized that it had barely tapped the vast universe of trusted untruths that exist just below the threshold of our awareness. I don't expect to exhaust the subject with this catalogue, only to share my observation that we are embedded in a boundless universe of claptrap, falsity, fakery, and artifice. Much is no doubt deceit, but at least as much is likely a different type of lie, growing out of inattention, the perseverance of old wives' tales and myths that refuse to die. My intent is to send as many as possible of these offenders off to their well-deserved banishment.

I knew the earlier volume was on its way to success when I received some considered letters from readers, most laudatory, a few censorious. One particular entry in the book drew a pair of potent objections to my characterization of a politically sensitive falsification. One was instructive, the other hostile. Some people, I discovered, are so wedded to their fallacious beliefs as to be threatened by the truth. Still, it was gratifying to learn that at least some readers were paying attention.

I must acknowledge the help of staff at several southern Westchester public libraries. Librarians are a rare breed, a group of professionals who are dedicated to spreading learning in a society that badly needs it. They are, for me, a constant source of enlightenment.

A note of recognition for a pair of colleagues whose involvement started late but proved useful, somewhat; I honor their preference for anonymity to avoid any blame for the final product. However, they know who they are. My gratitude for my daughter Liza's counseling, her useful suggestions, and, while reading the text, her barely suppressed chuckle every time she tracked down and corrected a misspelling or an awkward phrase. And my appreciation for the participation of seventeen-year-old Jordyn Ecoff who contributed to the inventory of parental falsehoods noted in the Foreword. Jordyn is not only a valued contributor, she is also my super-valued granddaughter.

I thank you all.

FOREWORD

Although we boast of American probity, in truth we are a country often contaminated by lies. We are brought up in lies, reared on untruths, and move into an adulthood governed by falsifications. (Witness the recent—2016—presidential campaign.) We start out being told that Santa Claus leaves us gifts on Christmas Eve, that the tooth fairy places money under our pillow in exchange for a lost tooth, and that there's a place in Heaven for the virtuous even as we are being corrupted. As children, we are bombarded with a glut of such falsehoods:

- When you lie, your forehead shows a red dot that can be seen only by your mother.
- If you don't eat your veggies, your teacher will know.
- A tube connects your bellybutton to your butt; if you unscrew your bellybutton your butt falls off.
- Step on a crack, break your mother's back.
- Your teacher has eyes in the back of her head and always knows what you're doing.
- Making a silly face will freeze that way.
- Daddy still loves you even though you used his razor to shave the cat.

When we move into adolescence we encounter another set of untruths, being told that our teachers are never wrong, our parents know best under any circumstances, cleanliness is next to godliness, and a whole new cluster of admonitions:

- Cracking your knuckles causes arthritis in the hands.
- Wait for an hour after eating before going into the pool.
- Eating chocolate gives you zits.
- Masturbation causes blindness.
- Spinach makes you strong.
- When I was your age, I walked three miles to school, uphill in both directions.

All this as today's parents are trying to raise their children to be honest, responsible citizens. Or so they say. Is it any wonder we learn early to bend the truth to our advantage, soon discover fibs, then misrepresentations, later outright lies. If it's not in the blood, it is in the culture. Or maybe in the genes of *Homo sapiens*.

Whatever the source of our information, it may not be apparent that much of it is erroneous. If we've not been intentionally lied to, we have often at least been misinformed. And so we remain throughout our lives. We carry around a vast inventory of knowledge that is simply wrong. And we share it with our colleagues. We may have gleaned it in school, at our job, from our chums, from the media, or from our parents. It may be widely accepted as fact, but much of it is untrue.

My intention, in the pages that follow, is to disabuse you of some of the fallacies you tolerate as facts. We will examine misbeliefs about history, government, current events, geography, sports, and pop culture, debunking the untruths they perpetuate. And, hopefully, set the record straight at least on some of the misconceptions you've believed for years.

Following the main part of the text are three short addenda—a section entitled "Who Says So?", a short selection of misattributed quotations, identifying the person who actually said what has been credited to another, if it was actually said at all; a section on "Experts and Naysayers," citing several examples of how authorities, leaders in their fields, can often make misleading pronouncements; and the final section on "Politicians"—*sine qua non* for a discussion of lying—reviewing some of their half-truths, nontruths, and other absurdities.

So be wary. Untruth is seldom indifferent. As Francis Bacon observed in his essay, "Of Vain-Glory": "Lies are sufficient to breed opinion and opinion brings on substance."

"It is easier to believe than to doubt."
        —E. D. Martin, in *The Meaning of a Liberal Education*

"We are incredibly heedless in the formation of our beliefs, but find ourselves filled with an illicit passion for them when anyone proposes to rob us of their companionship."
        —James Harvey Robinson, in *The Mind in the Making*

Lies, Half-Truths, and More Lies

SECTION ONE:
WHAT CAN WE BELIEVE?

A KKK SUPREME COURT JUSTICE?

{ Obviously, no member of the Ku Klux Klan has ever achieved a seat on the US Supreme Court.
Don't you believe it. }

Hugo Black was a senator from Alabama when he was appointed Associate Justice of the Supreme Court by President Roosevelt in 1937. After being confirmed by the Senate he publicly admitted that he had been a member of the Ku Klux Klan.

A native Alabaman, Black had graduated Phi Beta Kappa from the University of Alabama Law School. He practiced law in Birmingham, where he also served as a police court magistrate (his only judicial experience before the Supreme Court). Developing political ambitions, he joined the KKK to broaden his political constituency, but resigned after two years, just before campaigning for a Senate seat in 1926. Later he said the Klan was a mistake, but "I would have joined any group if it helped get me votes."

When a vacancy occurred on the Supreme Court, President Roosevelt wanted to fill it with a "thumping, evangelical New Dealer," reasonably young, and from a part of the country unrepresented on the Court. Black had all the qualifications, and as a senator had voted for all of Roosevelt's New Deal programs. Though from a Southern state, Black early demonstrated his support for liberal policies and civil liberties.

He endorsed Roosevelt in the 1932 and 1936 presidential elections, and was a staunch advocate for the New Deal. Black believed in stringent adherence to the First Amendment. In addition to voting in *Brown v. Board of Education* against segregation in public schools, in several decisions Black came down on to strict separation of church and state; he voted against religious instruction or official prayers in public schools. And he voted to permit publication of the Pentagon Papers.

UNDERAGE CONGRESSMEN

{ The United States Congress makes the laws of the nation, so one would assume it adheres strictly to Constitutional dictates.
Don't you believe it. }

There are specific requirements for serving in Congress. The Constitution explicitly codifies minimum age and residency for both senators and representatives. Concerning the Senate, for example, Section 3 of Article 1 says, "No Person shall be a Senator who shall not have attained the Age of thirty Years, and have been nine Years a Citizen of the United States."

It couldn't be clearer: No one under thirty may be a senator. At least so says the Constitution. But—against its own rules—in the early 1800s four men served in the Senate while not of the required age—two only twenty-eight years old, and two twenty-nine. Sources disagree which was the youngest, some naming John Henry Eaton of Tennessee, who served from 1818 to 1829, some choosing Armistead Thomson Mason of Virginia, senator from 1816 to 1817. Governmental records are more exact, showing that Mason was twenty-eight years and five months when he took office, Eaton twenty-eight years and three months, marking Eaton the younger. It has been speculated that such divergences from Constitutional requirements reflected either the insufficiency of records at the time, or possibly that the honored one may have actually not known his own birthdate. Or, of course, the Senate governance may have been slipshod.

The record of the House of Representatives is no better. The Constitution set the minimum age at twenty-five for Representatives, but the *Biographical Directory of the United States Congress* names four younger who served in the House, the youngest William C. C. Claiborne of Tennessee, elected in June 1797 at age twenty-two.

So Congress has offended the Constitution at least eight times.

GUNFIGHT AT THE O. K. CORRAL

{ Wyatt Earp and his brothers, along with their friend Doc Holliday, confronted the Clanton brothers, capping a long-standing feud, in a shoot-out at the O. K. Corral in Tombstone, Arizona.
Don't you believe it. }

In the 1880s the Arizona Territory was rife with cattle rustling and other outlaw activity. One of the towns that profited from such doings was Tombstone, where the Clanton and McLaury clans owned ranches reputed to be dealing in stolen cattle. The marshal of Tombstone was Virgil Earp, his brother Morgan was his assistant marshal, and Wyatt was his deputy; Wyatt planned to run for county sheriff in the upcoming election.

A clash developed between the opposing families for control of the town, the Earps wearing the white hats, the Clantons and McLaurys wearing the black. The hostility came to a head on October 26, 1881, when the two groups faced off in a thirty-second shoot-out, the Earps supported by their friend Doc Holliday, the Clantons and McLaurys augmented by cowboy Billy Claiborne. Unlike the sniping from behind protective structures as staged in the Burt Lancaster/Kirk Douglas film, the opposing sides stood barely six feet apart and blasted one another up close. About thirty shots were fired.

Billy Clanton and both McLaury brothers were killed, Virgil Earp, Morgan Wyatt, and Doc Holliday were wounded, while Wyatt Earp was not hurt.

But despite the label naming the event, the encounter did not take place in the O.K. Corral, or even adjacent to it. The confrontation actually occurred about a half-block away from the rear entrance to the O. K. Corral in an alley adjoining a photographic studio on Fremont Street. But calling the event "The Gunfight In An Alley Next to a Photographic Studio" just isn't as dramatic.

THE FOUNDING FATHERS

Being strong-willed men of firm opinion, our Founding Fathers were bound to encounter Intellectual disagreements as they confronted their diverse perspectives on creating a new nation. But as men of uncommon complaisance and refinement—men on a grand mission—their disagreements were no doubt tempered by their mutual respect and civility, as befitting the gentlemen they were.
Don't you believe it.

Political discourse at the time of the nation's inception was not as genteel as might be imagined. As Pulitzer-Prize winning historian/biographer Ron Chernow has observed, "For sheer verbal savagery, the founding fathers may have surpassed anything seen today." Men on a grand mission, certainly, but nonetheless men, with all the biases, vexations, incongruities, resentments, and inanities appurtenant to their humanness. Their disputations may have been eloquent, and their contemplations may have been on a lofty plain, at least sometimes, but their assessments of their fellows did not always reflect the same level of tolerance.

For example, consider John Adams's opinion of Jefferson: "I am obliged to look upon [Jefferson] as a man whose mind is warped by prejudice and so blinded by ignorance as to be unfit for the office he holds. However wise and scientific as philosopher, as a politician he is a child and dupe of party." And elsewhere: "His soul is poisoned with ambition." Or Jefferson's take on Adams: "[Adams] is vain, irritable and a bad calculator of the force and probable effect of the motives which govern men."

Or Hamilton's appraisal of John Adams: "[Adams] does not possess the talents adapted to the administration of government . . . there are great and intrinsic defects in his character . . . He is often liable to paroxysms of anger, which deprive him of self-command and produce very outrageous behavior . . ." Or Adams's view of Hamilton: an "insolent coxcomb who rarely dined in good company." Or, elsewhere: "That bastard brat of a Scottish peddler! His ambition, his restlessness and his grandiose schemes come, I'm convinced, from a superabundance of secretions, which he couldn't find enough whores to absorb!"

Or Jefferson's comments about Hamilton: "Hamilton was, Indeed, a singular character . . . bewitched and perverted by the British example—as to be under thorough conviction that corruption was essential to the government of a nation." Or, elsewhere: "When this government was first established, it was possible to have kept it going on true principle, but . . . Hamilton destroyed that hope in the bud."

Or Aaron Burr's assessment of James Monroe: "Naturally dull and stupid; extremely illiterate; indecisive to a degree that would be incredible to one who did not know; pusillanimous, and, of course, hypocritical; [he] has no opinion on any subject. . ." Or Thomas Paine's charge that Washington was "treacherous in private friendship . . . and a hypocrite in public life," wondering aloud whether Washington was "an apostate or an imposter."

Or Franklin's opinion of John Adams: "[Adams] means well for his country, is always an honest man, often a wise one, but sometimes, and in some things, absolutely out of his senses." Add to that Adams's caustic comments on everyone in his circle: on Washington: "That Washington is not a scholar is certain. That he is illiterate, unlearned, unread for his station is equally beyond dispute." Or on Franklin: "His whole life has been one continued insult to good manners and to decency."

And last, one of Hamilton's comments about Burr that led to the duel that ended Hamilton's life: "[Burr is] a dangerous man and one who ought not to be trusted with the reins of government."

So much for the tolerant, honorable gentlemen who gave birth to our nation.

NOAH

Noah, we remember, was instructed by the Lord to save a pair of every different kind of animal on earth—one male and one female—by bringing them onto the ark until the impending flood had ended and the waters receded.
Don't you believe it.

If you are really familiar with your Bible you will recognize that it was not all quite that simple. Despite what has been portrayed in the movies and in dozens of children's primers, it is not certain that all animals were to be boarded in pairs. Genesis 7.8–9 tells us that "Of clean beasts, and of beasts that are not clean, and of fowls, and of every thing that creepeth upon the earth, There went in two and two unto Noah into the ark, the male and the female, as God had commanded Noah."

However, and herein lies the problem, a bit earlier, in Genesis 7.2–3, we learn that the Lord told Noah, "Of every clean beast thou shalt take to thee by sevens, the male and the female: and of beasts that are not clean by two, the male and his female. Of fowls also of the air by sevens, the male and the female . . ." If I were Noah, I would be rather perplexed by these contradictory instructions.

But that's not all of it. Genesis 7.14–15 adds to the confusion: ". . . .very beast after his kind, and all the cattle after their kind, and every creeping thing that creepeth upon the earth after his kind, and every foul after his kind, every bird of every sort. And they that went in unto Noah into the ark, two and two of all flesh, wherein is the breath of life. And they that went in, went in male and female of all flesh, as God had commanded him . . ." Confirming one dictate, refuting another.

There are other conflicting passages in the Bible, but none in this proximity.

SARDINES

> Sardines are delicious little fish, caught in massive numbers because they travel in large schools, easy to net in several waters around the globe.
> **Don't you believe it.**

There is no such fish as the sardine. It is a designation used for several diminutive, oily fish of the herring family of clupeidae. But their definition varies around the world. In some classifications, notably the United Kingdom's Sea Fish Industry Authority, sardines are codified simply as young pilchards.

The *Codex Alimentarius*, developed by the UN's Food and Agricultural Organization and the World Health Organization, contains a standard for canned sardines that identifies twenty-one species that can be categorized as sardines. And some other authorities restrict the sardine appellation only to small fish when packed in cans, likely in oil, but sometimes in tomato sauce, in various spices, or simply in water.

Notably nutritious, sardines are a widely used foodstuff, are very high in omega-3 fatty acids EPA and DHA, both of which are known to lower levels of cholesterol and triglycerides, and are also rich in vitamin B_{12}; all of these attributes are known to promote cardiovascular health. They are also an excellent source of vitamin D, important because we no longer spend much time outdoors in natural sunlight, and of minerals selenium, phosphorus, and calcium. A standard can of 3.75 ounces contains only 200 calories.

They are especially handy as a reserve snack when traveling–the cans are easy to pack or carry, lightweight and leakproof. And the fish require no preparation, unless you feel the need to dress them up. They can be eaten fresh out of the can, with or without accompaniment, in a sandwich, salted, smoked, mashed, or added to tomato sauce over spaghetti. Or grilled crisp and added to your favorite salad.

A curious fish, or fishes.

First Blood
at Pearl Harbor

{ It is well known that the December 1941 Japanese attack on Pearl Harbor propelled the United States into World War II. But not well known is that the first blood that day was drawn not by the Japanese, but by American naval forces.
You can believe it. }

At 0358 on the morning of December 7 the destroyer *Ward*, on patrol off the entrance to Pearl Harbor, received a signal that the minesweeper *Condor* that had sighted an object looking like a periscope. The *Ward*'s skipper, Lt. William Outerbridge, was unable to locate a submarine and at 0443 he secured from general quarters. Later, at about 0630, a PBY patrol plane reported a submarine tailing a cargo ship, the USS *Antares*. The *Ward* soon spotted the sub and fired when it got close enough, registering a direct hit. At least that was what the crew believed and boasted about.

Outerbridge, who had taken command of the ship less than twenty-four hours before his patrol set off, wired Pearl at 0653, "Attacked, fired upon, depth bombed, and sunk submarine operating in defensive sea area." This was just over an hour before the first Japanese planes began their bombing runs. Authorities were slow to accept the account because a number of similar reports had been received and shown to be spurious; also, no physical proof existed.

For several years the kill remained unconfirmed and the action stayed on the records as a "maybe." Then, in August 2002, researchers from the Hawaii Undersea Research Laboratory found a miniature sub at 1,200 feet some three-to-four miles off Pearl Harbor. The deck gunners on the Ward had claimed they hit the sub at the base of the conning tower and that's what the undersea researchers found.

Confirmation was finally established sixty-one years later. America had drawn first blood.

VALLEY FORGE

{ The winter Colonial forces camped at Valley Forge was the coldest in several years. Many died from the sub-zero weather.
Don't you believe it. }

The Valley Forge Historical Society lists the winter of 1777–78 as a moderate winter, not unusually frigid. Yet, many soldiers couldn't take the cold and dozens deserted. There were 2,000 deaths, but most were during the warmer months of March through May, and from diseases like influenza, dysentery, typhoid, and typhus.

Food and clothing were in short supply. The reports of some soldiers being naked didn't mean they had no clothes; in military terms it meant they lacked proper uniforms and were therefore unfit for duty. But nevertheless warm clothing was scarce.

The encampment saw two stretches of extreme cold: A low of 6 degrees at the end of December and 8 degrees and the end of March. A heavy snowfall hit on February 8, but it was washed away by heavy rainfall in the next few days. None of the three extended snowstorms reached blizzard intensity. Records show that between the nasty periods there were stretches of above-average temperature. With a shortage of proper clothing and adequate housing, it was a tough winter, but not the disastrous Siberia we have been taught about.

By February the weather improved. By March food and supplies began showing up. By April, Baron von Steuben, a former Prussian army officer, had begun training the threadbare troops to become a solid fighting force. As they became more adept and battle-ready, their morale was much improved. The unruly mob that arrived in December 1777 decamped on June 19, 1778, a proficient and confident fighting force.

Nine days later the Colonials met the British in the Battle of Monmouth, where Washington's forces fought the British to a standstill.

BOYCOTT

{ The group practice of abstaining from, or preventing dealings with, as a means of coercion, named for the man who first practiced it.
Don't you believe it. }

Yes, the word defines the process of refraining from contact with a person or a group or a business or an organization. But no, it is not named after its first practitioner, but rather its first victim.

The late 1870s saw catastrophic crop failures in Ireland, causing widespread famine. Thousands of farmers were unable to meet their rents due English landlords and they offered partial payment to demonstrate their good intentions. Aware of their tenants' financial problems, many landlords accepted the offer, but not Lord Erne, who owned several properties in County Mayo. Rather, he instructed his local agent, Captain Charles Boycott, to collect the rents using whatever means he thought necessary.

About 3,000 farmers were at risk and Boycott showed them no leniency, often demonstrating ruthless dedication to his assigned task. But he wasn't prepared for the depth of Irish anger and the people's determination to finally free themselves from English shackles. Rather than being intimidated, the farmers decided to pay no rent at all; they stopped working the land and formed the Irish Land League. And they refused to have any further dealings with Captain Boycott. The movement spread, gaining adherents, hostility grew, and even his servants revolted. Attempts were made to close down his food supply.

In order to regain control, several dozen Orangemen from Northern Ireland were sent to Mayo, protected by 1,000 soldiers. There they harvested what remained of the crop and rescued Boycott, who escaped to England where he died in 1897, having given his name to a new way to dispose of unwanted relationships.

THE LAS VEGAS STRIP

Las Vegas is America's party city. And nowhere is the party more exuberant than on the world-renowned Las Vegas Strip, that section of the city that boasts most of the city's grand hotels, casinos, and resort venues.
Don't you believe it.

Yes, Las Vegas is the fabled all-night Nevada city where anything goes, including the money you arrived with. But the Las Vegas Strip, in spite of an almost universal misconception, is not in the city of Las Vegas.

The Strip is a stretch of Las Vegas Boulevard that begins immediately south of the Vegas city limits and extends into the unincorporated towns of Paradise and Winchester. Spanning slightly over four miles, it contains many of the world's largest hotels and resort properties. Wikipedia estimates that fifteen of the world's largest twenty-five hotels by room count are on the Strip, with a total of 62,000 rooms.

Many are theme hotels, representing some of the planet's most recognizable tourist attractions; a world of counterfeit replicas, such as a half-size Eiffel tower at the Paris Las Vegas, a faux pirate ship at the Treasure Island, a Disney-inspired replica of the Sphinx along with sham pyramids at the Luxor, even gondola rides on pretend canals at the Venetian. And fountains, everywhere fountains. It's difficult to believe it's all in the middle of a desert.

Suggesting an adult Fantasyland, the Strip has been lauded by some commentators for its "dramatic architecture," while others have recoiled in horror at the amusement-park sensibility they see in the corridor of disgracefully flamboyant, often bizarrely baroque, hotels, and gambling casinos. But none of it is within the city's boundaries.

TRANSMUTATION

{
Medieval alchemists were obsessed with finding the philosopher's stone, a substance believed to govern the process of chrysopoeia, turning base metals (such as lead) into noble metals (such as gold). But by the 1720s the search was abandoned and transmutation was considered impossible.
Don't you believe it.
}

The study of alchemy dates back to ancient Egypt. But the search for chrysopoeia intensified in the Middle Ages and into the Renaissance. Even some renowned scientists dabbled in alchemy, notably Robert Boyle and Isaac Newton. Alchemists tried hundreds of chemical combinations attempting to produce gold. Until early in the eighteenth century, when alchemy and chemistry became differentiated.

The philosopher's stone was recognized as myth, alchemists came to be seen as pseudoscientific charlatans, and transmutation was deemed unattainable.

But with the twentieth century's atomic age, transmutation of elements became possible. Some ten years after Becquerel discovered radioactivity in 1896, physicist Ernest Rutherford and chemist Frederick Soddy, analyzing emissions of radioactive substances, found that thorium disintegrated into argon gas. They realized that radioactive disintegration involved the spontaneous transmutation of one chemical element to another. Nowadays nuclear physicists routinely accomplish it.

But what of turning lead into gold? Striking a lead target with high-speed nuclei in a particle accelerator would produce the transmutation. Glenn Seaborg, chemistry Nobel Prize winner, who successfully transmuted gold from bismuth, agrees that it could be done, but "would cost more than one quadrillion dollars per ounce to produce gold by this experiment." Considerably more than the market price.

But it can be done.

MISSING DAYS

{ The days from September 3–13 in the year 1752 vanished. They ceased to be on our calendar. **You can believe it.** }

In the year 1752 the sun set on the British Empire on September 2, and when it rose the following day it was September 14. What happened to the intervening days?

The Western World, i.e. the Christian world, had switched from the Julian calendar to the Gregorian calendar, eliminating several days. The Julian calendar, introduced by Julius Caesar in the year 45 BC, defined a year of 365 days, six hours. But the solar year is actually 365 days, five hours, forty-eight minutes, and forty-six seconds (365.256 days). The two were not in sync, off by less than twelve minutes, but by the sixth century Easter, traditionally observed on March 21, had diverged noticeably from the vernal equinox.

So in 1582 Pope Gregory XIII ordained that ten days be dropped and he inaugurated the new calendar to better conform to the regularity of seasonal change. But non-Catholic countries were slow in accepting the Gregorian calendar and it wasn't adopted in Britain and its colonies until 1752, by which time the variance had become eleven days. That's when we made the change.

Still, every fourth year we add an additional day to the end of February, creating what we call a leap year. But that makes the year too long, so we eliminate February 29 in every hundredth year, but include it in years divisible by 400. Unwieldy, but it solves the problem . . . almost. This solution still leaves a twenty-six-second divergence for the Gregorian calendar from the solar year. Which will cumulate over time and likely require another adjustment some time in the future.

Yet, other minor adjustments are needed; for example, every now and then a leap second must be added to account for the Earth's ever slowing rotation. Confused?

THE BORDER STATES

{
The 1850s witnessed increasing contention between the North and the South over the issue of slavery. In response to Lincoln's election to the presidency in 1860, all slave-holding states seceded from the Union to form the Confederate States of America.
Don't you believe it.
}

Not all of the slave states seceded. At the beginning of 1861 the United States comprised thirty-four states. After Lincoln's election, but before his inauguration in March 1861, seven of the slave-holding states in the Deep South—Alabama, Florida, Georgia, Louisiana, Mississippi, South Carolina, and Texas—declared their secession and established the Confederate States of America. Eight slave states did not follow, until, that is, Fort Sumter fell and Lincoln called for action "to suppress" what he saw as a rebellion against the authority of the federal government. His request for 75,000 militiamen to recapture Fort Sumter and other government assets was seen by many as attempted military coercion of the South and swayed four of the uncommitted states—Arkansas, North Carolina, Tennessee, and Virginia—to then join the Confederacy.

The other four—those we know as the "border states" positioned between the Northern and Southern clusters—did not secede but remained in the Union: Delaware, Kentucky, Maryland, and Missouri. Also classified as a border state is West Virginia, formed from the western counties of Virginia that had cut loose and became a new state in the Union in 1863.

The border states suffered serious internal dissension, as they harbored both active pro-Confederate and pro-Union factions who daily lived side-by-side in opposition. Sometimes members of the same family fought on opposite sides. Nonetheless, these states did not secede from the Union.

THE CHAMPAGNE PUNT

{ The deep indentation at the bottom of a champagne bottle is designed to increase profits by limiting the amount of bubbly in the bottle.
Don't you believe it. }

Actually, that indentation, called the "punt," serves as a practicality. There are several reasons for it, none of which involves cheating the buyer, even though the indent adds weight and necessitates a taller bottle, both giving the impression that more liquid is contained.

One reason relates to the way bottles are stored, traditionally lying horizontal to aid the process of fermentation and to keep the cork moist so it doesn't shrivel up and fall inside. Lying the bottles end to end, with the cork of one placed in the punt of another saves space by allowing more bottles on each shelf or bin. Or, if stored top down, the insertion is still a space saver.

Then consider the way the bottle is handled. The pit on the bottom makes pouring easier, with the thumb in the indent and fingers outside. Grasping the bottle by the bottom prevents the warmth of the hand from being transferred inside and changing the temperature of the chilled wine.

Producing champagne entails a second fermentation to foster carbonation, creating carbon dioxide gas. Pressure built up in the bottle must be contained. We know how stored gas ejects the cork when the bottle is opened. The indentation strengthens the glass, supporting the structural integrity of the bottle.

The rim around the bottom steadies the standing bottle. A flat bottom is likely to be slightly rounded and thus less sturdy.

Also, the addition of a punt increases the surface area of the bottle, which quickens chilling the contents. Further, the channels inside, around the indent, collect residue that is less likely to blend back into the liquid when it's poured.

GANDHI

{ Mahatma Gandhi, recognized in India as the "Father
of Our Nation," is known for his strategy of nonvio-
lent protest, a lifelong belief that characterized his
struggle for Indian independence from British rule.
Don't you believe it. }

His name was Mohandas, not Mahatma. Mahatma is not a
name; it's a title of respect. And he was not always a proponent of
nonviolence. In the Boer War and the 1906 war with the Zulus,
he helped recruit Indians to serve as stretcher-bearers supporting
the armed troops. In the First World War he agreed to recruit
Indians for combat service.

Gandhi was usually photographed in public, even at formal
events, with legs bared, wearing what appeared to be a sheet. He
preferred dressing in his native costume. In many ways a paragon
of a virtuous model citizen, Gandhi was also a strange old geezer.

In his later years he had a habit of sleeping in the nude with
naked young women. But his proclivity was not born of lust, rather
as a way of testing his vow of chastity. Or so he said. What his
biographers don't tell us is whether he ever failed the test. He was
also against ejaculation, maintaining that retention of the "vital
liquid" was necessary to maintain energy and strength. His advice
to newlyweds was to stay celibate for the sake of their souls.

He was also big on bowel movements, especially the useful-
ness of the clyster, more commonly known as the enema. He is
believed to have had one every day. He is also reputed to have
greeted his young ladies with, "Have you had good bowel movement this morning?"

Not much of a family man, Gandhi refused to let his wife or
his sons get an education. When he disapproved of his oldest son's
marriage, he disowned him.

A strange old geezer indeed.

ALEXANDER HAMILTON
SEX SCANDAL

{
The sex scandal is a recent creation, aided by the growth of mass media. Our founding fathers certainly had their share of affairs, but generally managed to keep them quiet.
Don't you believe it.
}

A juicy scandal will make news even in the absence of radio, TV, and supermarket tabloids. For example, consider Alexander Hamilton's 1791 affair. The married thirty-six-year-old Hamilton met Maria Reynolds, a young Philadelphia woman who claimed that her husband had abandoned her and her child, and that she needed money to return to her family in New York. Hamilton agreed to help her. But the relationship soon metamorphosed into a two-year romantic liaison.

However Maria Reynolds was no forsaken waif. It is likely she and her husband James had plotted the affair to extort money from Hamilton, who was then Secretary of the Treasury. Reynolds demanded payment to keep quiet and Hamilton yielded, repetitively.

When Reynolds was caught in another scam, he used his knowledge about Hamilton's affair to bargain his way out, telling investigators that Hamilton was using government funds to pay hush money. When they confronted Hamilton about the charge he admitted the affair, showing them Maria's love letters. But he convinced them that the payoffs came from his own funds.

That should have ended the matter. But investigator James Monroe gave the letters to his friend Thomas Jefferson, Hamilton's fiercest political enemy. Jefferson handed them over to gossip-monger James Callender who, five years later, exposed the affair and printed the letters. Hamilton published his own version of the affair, admitting all. He was widely commended for his probity, but his political career never recovered.

So ended what was probably the nation's first sex scandal.

THE TOKYO FIREBOMBING

{ The atomic bombings of Hiroshima and Naga-
saki were the most destructive air strikes against
Japan during WWII, causing the most deaths and
destroying the most property.
Don't you believe it. }

The atomic bombings did enough severe damage to Japanese
infrastructure and Japanese morale to prompt Japan's uncondi-
tional surrender. But neither was the most destructive air action
against the island nation in World War II. Five months before the
first atomic bomb was dropped, the Operation Meetinghouse air
raid sent more than 300 B-29s over Tokyo on March 9–10, 1945.
The air armada released 1,665 tons of incendiary bombs on the
city, producing more devastation than either atomic attack. Estimates of fatalities varied from 90,000 to 125,000, almost equal
to the total number killed on site by both atom bombs.

General Curtis LeMay, in charge of strategic bombing in the
Pacific theatre of World War II, reasoned that since most of the
structures in Tokyo were made of wood, incendiary bombs would
likely do more damage than explosive devices, of any size. His plan
for called for the bombers to attack at night, when Japanese inter-
ceptor fighters were least capable, and from relatively low altitude
because their air defense ordnance was ineffective against low-
flying planes. The weapons used were mostly 500-pound cluster
bombs, each releasing a number of napalm-carrying incendiary
bomblets, designed to spread ruinous fire that would expand to
produce widespread incineration.

Operation Meetinghouse made over a million people homeless and obliterated 15.8 square miles of the city, compared with
five square miles destroyed by the Hiroshima explosion. The raid
was later estimated to be the most damaging air strike of the war,
and possibly the most damaging ever.

PINEAPPLES

> One of the delights of Hawaiian food, and drink, is its pineapple. Both sweet and slightly tart, the pineapple is one of Hawaii's favorite native fruits.
> **Don't you believe it.**

Though widely used in Hawaiian cuisine, and in several mixed drinks popular on the Islands (piña colada, etc.), the pineapple is not an indigenous fruit. Its source is not known for certain, but botanists believe it originally came from the South American region where Argentina, Paraguay, and Brazil meet. It is thought to have been brought to Hawaii about 1790 by Spanish sailor Don Francisco de Paula Marin, who served as translator for King Kamehameha I and was an accomplished horticulturist. According to Smithsonian records, Marin provided the first mention of the fruit on the islands in his January 1893 diary entry: "This day I planted pineapples and an orange tree."

In 1901 James Dole started the Hawaiian Pineapple Company and opened his first plantation on the Hawaiian island of Oahu. In 1922, Dole, the president of the company (later renamed Dole Food Company), bought the island of Lanai and converted a major portion of it into the world's largest pineapple plantation. Later, he built a canning plant. Small wonder that people believed the pineapple was a local accomplishment—born, raised, and refined in Hawaii.

Until, that is, the early 1960s, when increasing costs made it economically necessary to move the operation to a less expensive locale. The Dole Company moved its primary growing and production facilities to Asia, notably the Philippines and Thailand, where labor costs were significantly lower. The last planting on Lanai was harvested in the 2000–01 season. Some production in Hawaii has been retained, but only for local distribution.

Nonetheless, Hawaii is still identified as the pineapple state.

QUICK ONES

Following are corrections of several fallacies, fictions, fancies, fables, fantasies, forgeries, figments, and other fabrications—all common knowledge, self-evident, requiring no extended explanation. And all wrong. My hope is to emend the reader's memory and rid it of at least some misconceptions.

A law degree is not a requirement in order to be appointed to the Supreme Court. In fact, there are no constitutional requirements for becoming a Supreme Court justice.

Priests were not always celibate. Peter, the first Pope, as well as many of the apostles, were married men. But by the fifth century other attitudes were developing. In AD 401, St. Augustine wrote, "Nothing is so powerful in drawing the spirit of a man downward as the caresses of a woman." It wasn't until the twelfth century that the church decided priests should be celibate. And it should be noted that the original meaning of "celibate" was unmarried, not sex-repressive.

Elephants do not drink through their trunks. An elephant sucks up water into its truck and then sprays it into its mouth.

It isn't the tryptophan in the Thanksgiving dinner turkey that makes you sleepy. It is used by the body to make serotonin, which the body then uses to produce melatonin, a hormone that helps control sleep cycles. Authorities believe that consuming large quantities of carbs and alcohol are more likely the real cause of off drowsiness after a big meal. Turkey has no more tryptophan than many other foods.

The caesarian section has nothing to do with Julius Caesar. The name comes from the word *caesus*, past participle of the Latin word *caedo*, which means to cut or hollow out.

Author Tennessee Williams wasn't from Tennessee. He was a native of Mississippi.

Galileo is said to have dropped two objects of significantly different weight from the Tower of Pisa and thereby proved that such dissimilar objects hit the ground at the same time, unaffected by their weight, shape, or size. Scholars disagree whether this actually happened, but if it did it wasn't the first time. Historians of science have traced this same demonstration to the early 1500s, recorded by Florentine Benedetto Varchi in the 1540s, decades before Galileo was born, and again in 1576 by mathematics professor Giuseppe Moletti of the University of Padua.

The English horn is neither English nor a horn. It is a wood-wind related to the oboe.

According to the Mormon religion, anyone who is not Mormon is called a "gentile." So in Utah, even Jews are considered Gentiles.

The peanut is not a nut. It is a member of the pea family. A nut is a fruit having a hard shell and as seed, which is usually edible, where the shell does not open to give up the seed. The peanut is a legume.

English is not the official language of the United States. The US does not have an official language, which helps it maintain its melting-pot character.

Ostriches do not hide by burying their heads in the sand. But they may sometimes burrow into it searching for drinking water. They have long strong legs that can kick powerfully if they are threatened, but they usually run away when attacked.

Oddly, it is possible for fish to drown. Like every other animal, fish need oxygen to live. They extract oxygen from the water through their gills. If water is short on oxygen or so polluted that the oxygen supply is compromised, the fish could drown.

DR. SPOCK CONVICTED

{ Dr. Benjamin Spock, well known pediatrician and author, was jailed for counseling evasion of the draft during the Vietnam War. **Don't you believe it.** }

Dr. Spock is renowned for his 1946 volume, *The Common Sense Book of Baby and Child Care,* which by his death in 1998 had sold over fifty million copies in its nine editions and had been translated into thirty-nine languages. The essential guidebook for parents and expectant parents for almost seventy years, it is the second best-selling book of the twentieth century after the Bible.

A pediatrician who studied psychoanalysis to better understand children and adolescents, Dr. Spock altered the way children are raised. His message to mothers was "Trust yourself. You know more than you think you do," and he invited parents to have confidence in their capacity to do what had to be done and to believe in their own instincts. Breaking with the doctrines of the time, Spock advised parents to reject harsh discipline and strict scheduling and be more affectionate. His advice has informed decades of childrearing.

But Benjamin Spock was also a dedicated antiwar activist. He was one of the sponsors of *A Call to Resist Illegitimate Authority,* tract in support of draft resistance and the right of servicemen to refuse "illegal and immoral orders." In 1967 he, Martin Luther King Jr., and entertainer Harry Belafonte, led 300,000 marchers to a protest at the UN headquarters in New York City against involvement in Vietnam, the largest antiwar demonstration until that time.

In 1968 he and three other pacifist protestors were found guilty of conspiring to "counsel, aid, and abet Selective Service registrants to evade military service and refuse to carry draft cards." His sentence was overturned on appeal.

He never was jailed.

THE VIRGIN QUEEN

{ Elizabeth I of England was known as the Virgin Queen. But was this designation warranted? **Don't you believe it.** }

Elizabeth, daughter of Henry VIII and Anne Boleyn, never married and so became known as the Virgin Queen. Historians do not know whether she was or wasn't, but most think not. Henry died in 1547. His widow Catherine Parr married Thomas Seymour and they took Elizabeth into their household. Thomas, age forty, was wont to "romp and horseplay" with the fourteen-year-old Elizabeth, possibly introducing her to sex. When Catherine died in childbirth in 1548, Seymour proposed to Elizabeth but was rebuffed. She was still only fourteen years of age.

When Elizabeth was crowned queen at age twenty-five, she maintained her friendship with her childhood companion Robert Dudley, with whom she may have been in love. When Dudley's wife Amy died under suspicious circumstances in September 1560, it was ruled an accident, but many believed Dudley had arranged it so he could marry the queen. Elizabeth considered it, but decided against under pressure from advisors.

Rumors abounded about her relationships with several figures: Dudley, Robert Devereux, Earl of Essex, and Francis, Duke of Anjou. No one knows if any affairs were consummated, but speculation was rife throughout her reign. She also had many suitors for her hand, including King Eric of Sweden, Archduke Charles of Austria, and the future King Henry III of France. She used her desirability for political gain, but never agreed to marriage.

Tudor historian Alison Weir believes that although Elizabeth's fondness for flirting generated rumors, "[She] was too much mistress of herself and too great a stateswoman to succumb to the temptations of illicit sex."

But we still don't know.

BIRDMAN OF ALCATRAZ

{
In 1962, in one of his more believable roles, Burt Lancaster plays Robert Stroud, a convicted murderer who maintains an aviary in his prison cell at Alcatraz. **Don't you believe it.**
}

The film, *The Birdman of Alcatraz*, is essentially true except for one critical fact: The title is a lie; it didn't happen at Alcatraz.

Robert Stroud was a pimp in Alaska who in 1909 had killed a local bartender for abusing one of his prostitutes, for which he was incarcerated in the federal prison in Washington State. He quickly acquired a rep as a violent, dangerous inmate who repeatedly had run-ins with prison staff and other cons, and in 1916 he killed a guard who had canceled a visit by his mother. He was convicted of first-degree murder and sentenced to hang. But his death sentence was rescinded, commuted to life imprisonment, and he was moved to solitary confinement at Leavenworth Penitentiary.

One day he chanced upon a wounded sparrow in the prison yard and he cared for it until it was able to fly off. He developed an expanding interest in birds as he started researching and collecting them in his cell. By 1933 he published *Diseases of Canaries*, establishing his credentials as an expert in avian pathology, reinforced by his finding cures for certain bird disorders. While at Leavenworth he was permitted to rear and sell birds, all with the approval of the prison-reform warden.

But prison staff discovered he was also brewing alcohol with the equipment permitted him for his bird research. He was shipped out to Alcatraz—where he was disallowed from continuing his bird research and from boarding them in his cell. Devoid of his birds and his research paraphernalia, Stroud switched his interests and wrote a history of the penal system.

JESSE OWENS'S OLYMPICS

{ When Jesse Owens won four gold medals at the 1936 Berlin Olympics Hitler ignored him, refusing to shake his hand to acknowledge him as a winner. **Don't you believe it.** }

The 1936 Olympics at Berlin were intended by Hitler to show off the supremacy of the Aryan race. German athletes were supposed to have command of the games and exhibit their racial superiority. But his expectations were smashed when a black athlete named Jesse Owens took four gold medals, all of which were meant to be won by exemplars of Hitler's master race; the coveted display of their superlative abilities was frustrated, as was he. Owens took gold in the 100-meter and 200-meter sprints, long jump, and the 4x100 meter relay, tying a world record and establishing new Olympic records for three others.

The previous year, at the Big Ten Conference Championships in Ann Arbor, Michigan, Owens had also broken three world records (long jump, 220-yard dash, and 220-yard low hurdles) and tied a fourth (100-yard dash), and all within a forty-five minute span, an accomplishment called by one observer "the greatest 45 minutes ever in sport."

But Hitler did not ignore him. True, der Führer did not shake his hand but, advised by the IOC chairman that it would violate Olympic protocol, he not shake any other hands either. Owens himself reported that, "When I passed the Chancellor he arose, waved his hand at me, and I waved back at him." Ironically, FDR, president at the time, did not invite Owens to the White House. "Hitler didn't snub me," Owens said, "it was our president who snubbed me. The president didn't even send me a telegram."

Owens, son of a sharecropper and grandson of a slave, was named James Cleveland by his parents, but when a teacher called him J. C. he became known as Jesse.

GEORGE WASHINGTON'S EXPENSE ACCOUNT

{ George Washington refused a salary for his service as commander-in-chief of the colonial army during the Revolutionary War.
True, but . . . }

Washington offered to lead the forces of the nascent American nation for no recompense other than reimbursement of his expenses. To that end he maintained an inventory of his outlays, neatly written in his own "fine Italian hand." It was originally published by the Treasury Department in June 1883 and rapidly achieved obscurity. Until, that is, it was rediscovered in the late 1960s by pseudo-historian Marvin Kitman, who authenticated it, edited it, wrote an exegesis, and published it in 1970 as *George Washington's Expense Account*. For this rendering the entries in pounds sterling were converted to dollars at the going rate of exchange.

It is an amazing document, foretelling the spending habits of today's expense-account class. For example, the first two entries set the tone for all later items; they total $7,644 for five horses and a top-of-the-line phaeton carriage "to equip me for my journey to the Army at Cambridge"—in other words, to take up his command. When the figures were analyzed in 1970 dollars, the cost of the carriage was the equivalent of roughly twelve Cadillac broughams.

Every time Washington traveled to consult with field staff at a different location, a charge was recorded in the vicinity of $1,000. Significant expenses were incurred whenever the General relocated his headquarters or moved the family lodgings nearer to his new location. The largest of these is shown as $27,665.30, "To Mrs. Washington's travell[ing] Exps. in coming to & returning from my Winter Quarters per accts. rendered." This exorbitant charge may have embarrassed even Washington; it is the only entry for which justification is provided.

Among recurrent entries are "Household Exps.," starting at a few hundred dollars per month in 1775, increasing to $1,000 then $2,000 in 1777, to $3,000 in 1778, to $4,000 in 1780, for a total over eight years of $157,330. Items all appear in general terms, a noticeably devoid of annotations. Which makes one item stand out even more: an entry of November 1775 lists several purchases of eggs, totaling more than thirty-four dozen in one month. Nobody can like eggs that much.

Other recurrent items include frequent entries for "Sundry Exps," again unexplained, amounts varying considerably, as much as $6,170 on June 18, 1778. Also vague "Secret Service" entries, each for several thousand dollars; and several charges of as much as $1,000 to replenish the wine supply, especially Washington's favored madeira, preferably the 1759 and 1763 vintages. Various entries record payments to unidentified names for unidentified purposes. Some appear to be loans to associates.

For the eight years the log was maintained, the account totals $449,261.51. At the same salary as other patriot generals the amount would have been $48,000. No one would accuse the father of our country of padding his expenses. Even though the temptation does present itself. But Kitman offers a more acceptable interpretation: "George Washington, it has been pointed out for centuries, was willing to make every sacrifice for liberty. Except one: reducing his standard of living."

When reviewed by a congressional committee, the General's figures were accepted in totality. They did find one error: a discrepancy of 89/90 of one dollar more was due Washington than his accounts showed. Apparently, the committee checked his arithmetic, not the validity of the charges.

But there is one more chapter to the story. When Washington was selected as the first president of the new country he proposed taking on the post on the same terms for which he fought the war—no salary, only expenses. Congress demurred.

JAPAN BOMBS THE US

{ Probably because of the defensive expanse of the Pacific Ocean, Japanese bombs never fell on the United States during the 1940s war with Japan. **Don't you believe it.** }

Several bombs did fall, but were kept out of the news both to prevent Americans from panicking and to keep the enemy unaware of its success. The bombs had been carried from Japan across the Pacific attached to balloons traveling on the westerly winds of the upper atmosphere, part of the Fu-go project. First deployed in November 1944, thousands of balloons were released into the upper jet stream, each carrying incendiary and explosive devices, designed to set ablaze the huge forests of the Pacific Northwest. Their mission was both to reduce American zeal for the war, and to divert resources from wartime to domestic activities.

The balloons were described as thirty-three feet in diameter with a load capacity of about 1,000 pounds, each carrying four incendiary devices and a thirty-three-pound anti-personnel fragmentation bomb. About 9,000 balloons were sent aloft, but only about 300 were confirmed to have landed in the US, as far north as upper Alaska, as far south as Nogales, Arizona, on the Mexican border, as far east as Farmington, Michigan, a few miles west of Detroit. Most did no damage at all.

The only casualties occurred on May 5, 1945, when a church pastor in Bly, Oregon, took five of his Sunday school class on a picnic. One of the children found a balloon and its attachments; it exploded while she was examining it, killing five children and the pastor's pregnant wife.

Seen by munitions experts as the first intercontinental weapon system, the Fu-go project was a military failure, producing minimal damage and having no effect on the war. After two balloons reversed course and landed in Japan, the program was canceled.

POISONED BOOZE

{ During Prohibition the government poisoned alcohol
to scare people into giving up illicit drinking.
You can believe it. }

Someone in the American government had the brilliant idea of adding poisonous methyl alcohol to drinkable ethyl alcohol to prevent people from imbibing it.

Before Prohibition potable ethyl alcohol, ethanol, was "denatured," that is, made impotable, by the addition of some adulterant that either tasted disgusting or produced serious stomach disorder. The intent was to prevent people from avoiding beverage taxes by drinking commercial-grade alcohol. But the denatured alcohol could be redistilled to make it consumable.

When Prohibition became law, the additives were increased, but people kept drinking. By the mid-1920s bootleggers were stealing millions of gallons of denatured industrial alcohol each year and making it borderline drinkable by distilling the contaminants out of it. By 1926 the quantities of stolen denatured alcohol were so enormous that the government changed its program. In place of the terrible tasting additives they started putting in more serious poisons. It was still possible to distill out the poison—or at least some of it—but the quality of the liquid suffered. That was when the cocktail became popular, fruit juice or some other additive serving to improve the taste. But the final product could still be toxic.

The idea of making liquor poisonous had its objectors. New Jersey Senator Edward I. Edwards called it "legalized murder." But Seymour M. Lowman, Assistant Secretary of the Treasury in charge of Prohibition, declared that if the result was a sober America, "a good job will have been done." Some supporters called it "a deliberate suicide."

Some 10,000 people died at the government's hands from the modified alcohol.

MAD AS A HATTER

{ The Mad Hatter, is a character in *Alice's Adventures in Wonderland* by Lewis Carroll. But is he merely a poetic metaphor? Or does he have some validity in real life?
You can believe it. }

Hat making, surprisingly, was once a dangerous occupation. The risk came from working with felt, a preferred material for headwear. The manufacture of felt involved the use of mercury, which can be destructive to the human body.

Most fabrics are woven, with fibers interlocked to create a flat cloth. Felt is not a textile; it is a dense, non-woven fabric made from wool, fur, or hair matted together by pressure, facilitated by heat and moisture. Wool is preferred, usual mixed with a synthetic to produce a strong, flexible, and resilient fabric perfect for such products as headwear. Felt can also be made entirely from synthetic materials.

Until the late nineteenth century mercury nitrate was used in curing felt for making hats. But it was found that prolonged exposure to the mercury vapors caused debilitating effects on the hatmaker, a form of poisoning that led to uncontrollable muscle tremors and twitching limbs, emotional instability, hallucinations, and other psychotic symptoms. So hatters really did go mad. The wearer was not at risk; by the time the hat was worn the vapors would have long been dispersed.

The phrase "mad as a hatter," or the more depictive "hatters' shakes," was in use decades before the appearance of Carroll's novel, associated in England with the felt hat trade by 1860. Similar symptoms were reported in Russia in 1829 and in France in 1869. In 1898 France passed a law protecting milliners from mercury exposures. In the United States, the mercury-based process was used until the early 1940s, when it was abandoned primarily because the metal was needed by the military for the manufacture of detonators.

STATUE OF LIBERTY

{ The Statue of Liberty was conceived as a gift to the United States from France, celebrating the two countries' joint dedication to freedom and liberty. **Don't you believe it.** }

The French government had nothing to do with the Statue, not in its conception, its fabrication, nor in its funding. It was the brainchild of sculptor Frédéric Auguste Bartholdi, who designed the Statue and sought financing to accomplish it. But it was not intended for the United States. The Statue was designed for Egypt, which Bartholdi had visited as a young man and where he was impressed by the Suez Canal in the midst of its construction. Energized, he proposed building a statue, of a size to rival the pyramids, meant to stand at one end of the Canal as a lighthouse.

The plan was never realized and Bartholdi turned his sights to the United States. The idea was for the French to finance the Statue and the Americans to choose its site and provide its platform. But the project proceeded slowly because funding was uncertain on both sides of the Atlantic. To raise money the completed torch-bearing arm was displayed at the Centennial Exposition in Philadelphia in 1876 and in Madison Square Park in Manhattan from 1876 to 1882. The head was exhibited at the 1878 Paris World's Fair.

Fully realized, the final Statue arrived in New York on June 7, 1885, but work on the foundation had stalled in need of finances. Publisher Joseph Pulitzer of the *New York World* picked up the cudgel and raised over $100,000 to complete the pedestal, which was finished in April 1886.

"The Statue of Liberty Enlightening the World" was dedicated on October 28, 1886, celebrated by New York's first ticker-tape parade and a dedication ceremony presided over by President Grover Cleveland.

But France was not the donor.

WOMAN FOR PRESIDENT

{ Hillary Rodham Clinton is the first woman candidate
for the presidency of the United States.
Don't you believe it. }

Several women have run for the office, some more seriously than others. On the lighter side, in 1940 Gracie Allen of the Burns and Allen comedy team announced her candidacy and performed many of the rituals, and even garnered the endorsement of Harvard University, but it was all a publicity stunt. Nonetheless, on Election Day she did receive a few hundred write-in votes. A number of other women have announced but failed to win their parties' nomination, most notably Democrat Shirley Chisholm of New York, the first African-American congresswoman, outvoted in favor of George McGovern at the 1972 national convention.

A few others did receive their party's nomination, but were ineligible because they didn't meet the Constitution's required minimum thirty-five years of age. Included here were Victoria Woodhull of the Equal Rights Party in 1872 and Linda Jenness of the Socialist Workers Party in 1972.

But there were those who did meet the requirements, secure their party's endorsement, and appear on official ballots. Belva Lockwood, distinguished as the first woman attorney to practice before the US Supreme Court, was the candidate of the National Equal Rights Party in 1884, and again in 1888. Oddly enough, in those years women could run for office but, before passage of the Nineteenth Amendment, still could not vote. Then, in 2012, and again in 2016, Jill Stein was the candidate of the Green Party.

Additionally, two women in recent decades have run on major party tickets for vice president: Democrat Geraldine Ferraro in 1984 and Republican Sarah Palin in 2008. Both lost.

BLACK THURSDAY

{ The day the stock market collapsed, setting off a worldwide depression, is known as Black Thursday. **Don't you believe it.** }

Thursday, October 24, 1929, was the day the market disaster began, but it wasn't a single-day event. The market opened at 305.85 that day and the Dow immediately dropped 11 percent, with volume three times the average. To support the market traders bought heavily and by the end of the day most of the loss had been recouped; the market closed down just 2 percent. The upswing continued the next day when the Dow regained another 1 percent to 301.22.

After the weekend, on Black Monday the Dow dropped to 260.64, a loss of 13 percent. The following day confirmed fears of investors that the high-flying days of stock speculation were over as another 12 percent was lost and panic set in. Investors ran. More than sixteen million shares were traded that day, the Dow closing at 230.07. Investors were wiped out as they had to liquidate their holdings or raise cash to meet their margin loans. People lost their confidence in the market, which had dropped 23 percent in just two days.

The buying frenzy of the 1920s was over and the market had lost $30 billion in value.

As the market tanked in the most devastating decline in US history, the American economy was shattered: wages fell over 40 percent, unemployment rose to 25 percent, economic growth came to a standstill. And it lasted throughout the 1930s. By 1933 unemployment was almost fifteen million people, 30 percent of the workforce. Close to half of America's banks had failed. Even with President's Roosevelt's New Deal programs, the American economy didn't get back to full swing until World War II.

But it didn't all happen on one day. Rather than remembering a Black Thursday, perhaps we should be memorializing a Black Week.

LOUIS PASTEUR

{
Louis Pasteur, world-renowned French chemist and microbiologist, was a model of the principled scientific researcher.
Don't you believe it.
}

We now know that Pasteur falsified research data and claimed credit for the work of other scientists. His published results were frequently at odds with his actual findings, and his experimental procedures were often not commensurate with good scientific method.

On the other hand, his groundbreaking discoveries of the principles of pasteurization, fermentation, and vaccination have had a major impact on society and the practice of medicine. He found that bacteria were responsible for souring beverages and he devised the process we now call pasteurization, during which microorganisms are destroyed by heating. For that he was credited with saving the French wine and beer industries. He also devised vaccines for rabies and anthrax. His research provided experimental support for the germ theory of disease and helped put an end to belief in spontaneous generation.

The importance of his contributions cannot be overestimated, but we now seem to overlook his scientific controversies with other researchers of his time. He made a lifelong enemy of Antoine Béchamp, one of France's most distinguished biologic researchers, when he usurped some of Béchamp's ideas and then deceptively demeaned Béchamp's contributions. Another antagonist was Jean Joseph Toussaint, a research veterinarian, from whom he "borrowed" a procedure, which he never credited, to develop his anthrax vaccine.

Much of the evidence for Pasteur's misdeeds came from his own laboratory notebooks, which he had directed never to be made public, but which were uncovered several years after his death.

MARCO POLO

{
Marco Polo, the first European to visit China, wrote about his solo trip in a book called *The Travels of Marco Polo*.
Don't you believe it.
}

He was neither the first nor a solo traveler; he was accompanied by his father Niccolò and his uncle Maffeo, both of whom had visited China previously. The title of the book in question was *Livre des Merveilles du Monde* (in English, *Book of the Marvels of the World*). *Travels of Marco Polo* is only a label for an English language version. And Polo didn't actually write it—he recounted his experiences to a cellmate in a Genoan prison.

Polo and his companions had left Venice for China in 1271, encouraged by the Great Khan who had earlier met Marco's father and uncle. Traveling part by sea and part overland on the Silk Road, they arrived at Kublai's court some three and a half years later, when Marco was twenty-one. He soon became a favorite of Kublai and was trusted with several assignments. The Polos returned to Venice in 1295.

Years later, Polo was captured in 1298 on a Venetian vessel in one of its recurrent wars with Genoa. He was held in a Genoan jail, locked up with Rustichello da Pisa, a writer, who transcribed Marco's stories about his travels and experiences in the court of Mongol ruler Kublai Khan. Rustichello added some implausible items of own, producing a document broadly true but with some questionable details.

Some skeptics doubt Polo ever got to China, but contrived his book from stories he had heard. They cite the absence of any reference to the Great Wall or chopsticks. They also note obvious incongruities in the text and the fact that Polo is nowhere mentioned in historic Chinese records. But most authorities accept that his detailed observations about Chinese daily life, culture, and geography could not have been learned anywhere else.

CONESTOGA WAGON

The conveyance that made it possible for pioneer families to move westward with enough supplies to sustain them over the long journey was a roomy, sturdy wagon that we have become familiar with through dozens of Western movies about the trek across the continent; it was called the Conestoga wagon.
Don't you believe it.

The storied Conestoga wagon was a distinctive type of vehicle, named for Conestoga, Pennsylvania, where it was first constructed. It was a heavy, broad-wheeled covered wagon used in Pennsylvania, its adjoining states, and Canada, designed to carry weighty cargo. The name was not generic for "covered wagon." Specifically, it was built with its floor curved upward at the ends to prevent its contents from spilling or falling out. And it was covered with sturdy canvas to protect the contents from the weather. The seams of the body were sealed with tar to prevent leakage when crossing rivers. Made for heavy payloads, the Condestoga wagon could support up to six tons.

But it was not the conveyance that moved settlers across the continent. It was too heavy and unwieldy to be pulled long distances. The wagon that helped settle the American West was the Prairie Schooner, a fanciful name for a common vehicle, an ordinary farm wagon with curved ribs added to support a protective cover. Popular through the nineteenth century, the prairie schooner was smaller and lighter than the Conestoga Wagon, with a flat floor and front wheels smaller than rear wheels to facilitate turning. Its name came from its appearance, its canvas top from a distance resembling the sails on a schooner on the prairie.

Both wagons fell out of use when the railroads were expanded to reach more of the country.

THE DEAD WINNER

{
In an episode in the ancient Olympic Games a competitor won an event even though he was dead. **You can believe it.**
}

The year was 564 BC, the competitor was Arrhichion of Phigalia, the event was the pankration (*pancratium* to the Romans), a combat sport without weapons and with virtually no rules, encompassing elements of boxing, wrestling, kicking, choking, and whatever else the competitors could think of to inflict physical damage.

The only moves disallowed were biting, gouging the opponent's eyes or other bodily orifices, and attacking the genitals. It was introduced into the Olympic games in 648 BC.

At the 54th Olympiad, Arrhichion was the defending champion in pankration, having won the event in the two previous Olympiads in 572 BC and 568 BC. As recounted by historians of the games, Arrhichion was locked in a strangle hold by his opponent (whose name has been lost to history) that he could not break but nonetheless refused to yield. According to the story, at this point his trainer called to him, "What a noble epitaph, 'He was never defeated at Olympia'." Arrhichion somehow managed to get off a kick dislocating either his opponent's toe or his ankle, depending on which version you prefer. But the sudden move broke his neck, causing his death, still in the hold of his adversary.

However, in the throes of unbearable pain, his opponent had signaled submission. Although he was dead, Arrhichion was proclaimed the victor. Talk about being dead set on winning.

The pankration, along with all Olympic events, was abolished in AD 393 by Emperor Theodosius I who, with his conversion to Christianity, felt impelled to do away with all pagan programs and activities. The Olympics were reborn in 1896 in Athens.

MONITOR VS. MERRIMACK

{
One of the most famous confrontations of the Civil War—the Battle of Hampton Roads—was fought on March 9, 1862, historically the first naval engagement between two ironclad warships, the *Monitor* for the North against the *Merrimack* for the South.
Don't you believe it.
}

There was no Confederate ship commissioned as the *Merrimack*. The Northern navy had previously floated a steam frigate named the *Merrimack*, but in 1860 it had been decommissioned for repair at the Norfolk Navy Yard in Virginia. It was still there when the war began in April 1861. To prevent its capture by the South, on April 20 Union sailors burned the ship to the waterline and sank her before evacuating the yard. But the Confederacy, desperately in need of ships, raised her, redesigned, and rebuilt her with heavy armor plating above the waterline, equipped her with powerful cannon, and rechristened her CSS *Virginia*. She was launched in February 1862, intent on destroying the wooden ships at the mouth of the James River and breaking the Union blockade.

On March 8, the *Virginia* lit into the Union fleet off Newport News, destroying several ships. The following morning the *Virginia* began to engage other Union vessels when the *Monitor* appeared and joined the battle. Both crews being poorly trained, their firing was ineffectual and not much damage was done on either side until *Monitor*'s bridge was hit, wounding the vessel's commander. The *Monitor* veered into shallow water, which the South took as its victory. It turned to renew its attack on the Union ships, but ran out of ammunition and went back to port.

The battle had very little effect on the Union blockade or the outcome of the war, but it did much to strengthen the South's morale.

THE WHITE FEATHER

{ The white feather as a symbol of cowardice originated with English women in World War I to stigmatize men who weren't in uniform and therefore shirking their military duty.
Don't you believe it. }

Yes, British women did award a white feather to men on the home front intended to suggest censure of those who weren't in the service. But its origins can be traced back many years before the war. There is evidence that the practice existed in the late eighteenth century, as witnessed by fiction and film, notably the 1902 novel, *The Four Feathers* by A. E. W. Mason, which was converted into at least seven films, and was featured in the first episode of the second season of the TV series, *Downtown Abbey,* in which ladies of the Order of the White Feather distribute feathers to the men who have not enlisted.

The source of this practice was thought to be a representation of the pale skin of a frightened face, from which the blood has drained in fear. But its origin is stranger than that. It dates back to the practice of cockfighting, in which a white feather characterized a bird ill-suited to the sport, one not courageous enough to participate. The plumage of a bird was taken to represent its bloodline and thus its courage. Pure-bred birds were known by their red and black feathers; any other color indicated a less distinguished lineage. The presence of even one white feather in a bird's tail hinted that the bird was crossbred.

Aficionados of the sport knew that only purebred cocks possessed the qualities that made a bird a good fighter. All others were "cowards," not fit for the cockpit. Therefore only birds with black or red plumage were trained as competitors; to "show the white feather" not only implied impure lineage but, generalizing, also signified cowards, both among cocks and men.

MORE QUICK ONES

It was not Columbus, but the explorer Ponce de Leon who was the first European to touch down in the United States. He arrived in what is now Florida on April 3, 1513, searching for the Fountain of Youth. Columbus landed in the Bahamas.

India ink isn't from India, rather from China. The French call it China ink.

On April 27, 1911, Wisconsin Congressman Victor Berge introduced a constitutional amendment to the House of Representatives intended to do away with . . . the Senate. The preamble read, "Whereras the Senate in particular has become an obstructive and useless body, a menace to the liberties of the people, and an obstacle to social growth." A congressional committee quickly buried the amendment.

Washington did not show much promise as a commander before the Revolution. In the French and Indian War, as a twenty-three-year-old Lt. Colonel, he was ordered to Ft. Duquesne in western Pennsylvania to purge the French from British territory. He and his 150 troops made a poor showing and were badly defeated. A year later, he was defeated once again when he returned serving under British General Edward Braddock, this time having two horses shot out from under him.

The Bible does not say that three wise men visited the baby Jesus, only that they brought three gifts (gold, frankincense, and myrrh). It does not say how many came by that day.

The funny bone is not a bone. Rather, it's a nerve, the ulnar nerve, which runs under the long bone in the upper arm called the humerus. Its length makes it particularly vulnerable to injury. Irritating the nerve creates a sensation like an electric shock. The name given to the bone is a pun on the symptom.

Florida is not the state nearest to Africa. Maine is. (Check your map.)

LADY GODIVA

{ Lady Godiva is reputed to have ridden naked on horseback through the streets of Coventry to repudiate the exorbitant taxes.
Maybe. Maybe not. }

Lady Godiva was the wife of Leofric, eleventh-century Earl of Mercia and Lord of Coventry. Leofric was ordered by King Edward to impose a large increase in taxes levied on the populace of Coventry. The aggrieved citizens appealed to the earl's good wife to help them and she requested her husband to lower the taxes. He at first refused, but she continued to implore him to reconsider until he finally responded that he would do so when she rode horseback naked through the center of the city, probably the eleventh-century equivalent of "When the cows come home."

Displaying a rare level of civic responsibility, the Lady is said to have done just that. After requesting the citizens of Coventry to remain indoors and not peek, she mounted her horse unclothed, covered by nothing but her long tresses, and rode her mount through the streets of the town. After her naked ride she reminded Leofric of his pledge; he proved to be good to his word and responded positively, turning back the taxes he had instituted earlier. The people became appreciative and the Lady became famous.

To this day, no one knows if this is myth or a real occurrence. We do know that there was a Godiva who married Leofric and that they lived in Coventry in the eleventh century. But there is neither confirmation nor refutation in the historic record. It may actually have happened. Or not.

A sidelight to the story involves a citizen named Thomas who, contravening the Lady's request, gave in to curiosity and decided to take a peek. He looked out his window when Godiva rode by and was immediately struck blind. Such was the origin of the character known as Peeping Tom.

KING ARTHUR

{ King Arthur is a sixth-century monarch of England, celebrated in Welsh poetry and legendary Arthurian romances. But did he really exist?
Don't you believe it. }

Much is written about King Arthur. He was a righteous monarch of Britain who defeated the Saxons in the late fifth and early sixth centuries. His queen was Guinevere. He ruled over an empire encompassing Britain, Ireland, Iceland, Norway and Gaul. He led a company of worthy knights who lived in Camelot and assembled at a renowned Round Table that was a wedding gift from his wife Guinevere's father, Leodegrance. The Round Table was symbolic of the equal status of all who attended.

The knights in Arthur's circle were the best in the kingdom, distinguished by their courage, honor, civility, and dignity. But one, Lancelot, unintentionally destroyed the brotherhood of the Knights of the Round Table when Guinevere fell in love with him and provoked a break between him and the king.

The events told of Arthur's rule are many and diverse, and they vary considerably depending on which historian recounts them. The elements of the stories are well known—the Wizard Merlin, Arthur's father Uther Pendragon, the sword Excalibur—but the accounts differ. There is no canonical history of the reign of Arthur.

In fact, Arthur may never have existed. The whole story may be myth, pure legend. Arthur is not mentioned in *The Anglo-Saxon Chronicle* (c. 890s), Bede's *Historia ecclesiastica gentis Anglorum* (*Ecclesiastical History of the English People*) (c. 731) or any other surviving historical work before 1800. Historian David Dumville spoke for most chroniclers when he said, "I think we can dispose of him quite briefly. . . .here is no historical evidence about Arthur . . ."

And yet, he may have been.

SIR THOMAS CRAPPER

{ It was a British plumber named Thomas Crapper who invented the flush toilet, for which he was knighted by Queen Victoria.
Don't you believe it. }

Here are two myths rolled into one, among the most ingrained of modern times. Thomas Crapper *was* a successful plumber in London, owner of the world's first bath, toilet, and sink showroom, but he did not invent the flush toilet and was not knighted by Queen Victoria, nor by any other royal. He did receive royal warrants from Prince Edward (who became Edward VII) and also from George V, both as Prince of Wales and later as king, any of which would have permitted him to use the title "royal sanitary engineer," but he was not a "sir."

Actually, the first flush toilet was created in 1596 by Sir John Harrington, a godson of Queen Elizabeth; it was installed in the palace for himself and the Queen. However, the device didn't catch on and Harrington never made another. Some 200 years later, Alexander Cummings re-invented it and in 1775 received the first patent for a flushing toilet, naming it the "water closet."

Nonetheless, Crapper gave his name to the common slang term for the device, popularized by doughboys serving in England who saw his name on his manufactured equipment and adopted the word "crapper" to mean "toilet." At least that's one credible theory.

The root of the word "crap," slang for human waste, is not so easy to trace. Several notions exist. It could have the same root, or could derive from the Middle English "crappe," an obsolete term that had been used in England to refer to rubbish or chaff.

Thomas Crapper did hold nine patents: Most for refinements to the toilet, including the floating petcock, but—alas!—not for a flush toilet.

FLAMMA

{
Roman gladiators might achieve freedom by winning several fights. It was something every gladiator wished for.
Don't you believe it.
}

Gladiators, slaves of the arena, spent their lives constantly at risk, fighting other gladiators, usually until one killed the other. But if a gladiator won enough fights he might be set free and awarded a special prize, a small wooden dagger known as the *rudis,* which symbolized his promotion from slave to free man. Few gladiators achieved such status.

One who earned this reward was named Flamma (The Flame), who became known as the Greatest Gladiator of All Time. In combat he fought as a *servitor,* a competitor armed with a small sword and shield. A *servitor* was usually pitted against a *retiarius,* who was armed with a long trident and a net.

Under Roman law, having been condemned to the arena, Flamma was a *servus poenae* (slave of the penalty), and was considered to be under sentence of death unless manumitted. Flamma, who had been a Syrian soldier captured in battle and condemned to death in gladiatorial combat, received the *rudis* four separate times, but never retired from the field.

He had attracted a following early on in his coliseum career and became a favorite contestant, establishing a reputation as a fearless combatant. Apparently he enjoyed the challenge of combat, for instead of taking advantage of his good fortune and leaving for a more comfortable life, he always returned to the arena. He eventually found death in the coliseum, but it not until thirteen years later.

His gravestone in Sicily includes his record: "Flamma, secutor, lived 30 years, fought 34 times, won 21 times, fought to a draw 9 times, defeated 4 times, a Syrian by nationality. Delicatus made this for his deserving comrade-in-arms."

Some guys just can't change.

AARON BURR'S TREASON

{ The Burr-Hamilton duel in 1804 was the result of a personal feud, but Aaron Burr remained an honorable man who proved his loyalty to the new nation. **Don't you believe it.** }

Burr was a United States senator in the 1790s, and our nation's third vice president, serving in Thomas Jefferson's first term. But the two did not get along. When Jefferson ran for re-election in 1804, Burr was not chosen to run with him again. Hamilton was influential in the decision to drop Burr from the ticket, which contributed to Burr's challenge to the duel. And we know how that turned out.

Having acquired no small amount of disrepute and no longer in government, Burr contemplated starting a colony under his own authority in the newly acquired Louisiana Territory. His motives were debated: no one knew if he was intent on enlarging the United States or founding an independent nation all his own. But his intention became suspect. He even approached the British ambassador about the prospect of his aligning with the British to take over the region and free it from the Union.

In late 1806 Burr led a small well-armed force down the Mississippi toward New Orleans. When the authorities began to investigate, a co-conspirator turned on Burr to save himself. On February 19, 1807, Burr was intercepted at what is now Alabama and escorted to Richmond to be tried for treason. He was acquitted in September because he hadn't engaged in an "overt act," as required by the Constitution for a finding of treason.

Nonetheless, the public saw him as a traitor, and he spent the next several years in Europe until returning to New York and his law practice in 1812. Burr suffered a debilitating stroke in 1834 and died in 1836, a broken and disgraced man.

WHO INFLUENCED WHOM?

{ European explorers believed that the primitive "Indians" would profit from adopting European beliefs and governing principles.
Don't you believe it. }

Several historians and social scientists have concluded that Native Americans taught their intruders at least as much as their intruders taught them. It was apparent that Native cultures were generally more peaceful, less belligerent, and more democratic than the societies that subjugated them. Historian and sociologist Professor James W. Loewen suggests that Native American ideas may have contributed to the democratic principles of our own government. The Native American concepts of liberty, equality, and fraternity, he proposes, engaged European social philosophers such as John Locke and Baron de Montesquieu, who then influenced our colonial leaders.

Loewen reports that historians have speculated that the extensive contact between colonists and members of the Iroquois League may have impacted our democracy more pointedly, the League illustrating how a sizeable domain could be governed democratically. Witness to intercolonial disputes, the Iroquois proposed that the colonies organize into a structure similar to that of the League. Benjamin Franklin, having had firsthand experience with the Iroquois, argued for the colonial powers to adopt such an organization: "It would be a strange thing if six nations of ignorant savages should be capable of forming a scheme for such a union and be able to execute it in such a manner as that it has subsisted ages and appears insoluble; and yet that a like union should be impracticable for ten or a dozen English colonies."

Franklin's advice was ignored. But later, when the Constitutional Convention was creating the master document, local Native American concepts were conspicuously part of the discussion.

HEDY LAMAAR

{ Hedy Lamaar, a Hollywood actress lauded for her exotic beauty, served the country by leading several war bond drives.
True, but much more. }

Hedy Lamaar, a world-renowned movie star, had a second, lesser-known life. As a performer she achieved early fame at the age of eighteen in a 1933 Czech-Austrian film titled *Ecstasy*, appearing naked in several settings and in a controversial simulated orgasm scene. Having attracted the attention of Hollywood's poohbahs, in 1937 she was contracted to MGM studios by Louis B. Mayer. Labeled as "the most beautiful woman in the world," she starred in such films as *Algiers* with Charles Boyer, *Comrade X* with Clark Gable, and *Samson and Delilah* with Victor Mature.

But Hedy Lamaar was not just another empty-headed Hollywood glamour girl. She was also a serious inventor who kept an architect's drafting table in her home. She invented an advanced type of traffic stoplight and a tablet that converted water into a carbonated drink. But she also contributed to military weaponry and wireless communications.

Torpedoes in WWII were erratic, easily deflected by ocean currents and averted by evasive maneuvers. Lamaar, working with composer George Antheil, saw the remedy in a torpedo that was radio controlled. But the radio signal could easily be jammed by the enemy. So they devised a system of spread-spectrum "frequency-hopping" in which the control signal jumped through a variety of random frequencies controlled by a sequencer. They patented the system in 1942 and gave it to the Navy.

Their technology persists in the US defense communications satellite system, and is basic to GPS, cellular phones, faxes, Wi-Fi networks, and other wireless communication.

In 2014, Hedy Lamaar was posthumously inducted into the National Inventors Hall of Fame.

Unelected President

> We've had several presidents who attained the position when their predecessor died during his term of office. But they all had been elected to the vice presidency, so their ascendency was no surprise.
> **Don't you believe it.**

Gerald Ford became the country's fortieth president on August 9, 1974, having been elected to neither the presidency nor the vice presidency. In his twenty-fifth year representing Michigan's 5th Congressional District, Ford was nominated vice president by President Nixon when Spiro Agnew resigned under allegations of bribery and income tax evasion. Ford was planning to retire from Congress when his thirteenth term in the House concluded in 1976, but his plans changed when President Nixon proposed him as replacement vice president under provision of the Twenty-Fifth Constitutional Amendment.

In the months that followed, Nixon became progressively embroiled in the Watergate scandal, culminating in his resignation on August 8, 1974. The following day Ford was sworn in as the thirty-eighth President of the United States, the first and only politico to achieve that office without being voted into either the presidency or vice presidency.

Upon assuming office, Ford nominated former New York Governor Nelson Rockefeller to fill the vice presidency that he had vacated and issued a presidential pardon for Nixon, which prompted several political observers to suspect that a deal had been made between them to protect Nixon from impeachment or indictment.

In 1976 Ford ran a reluctant campaign for re-election, first a closely fought primary against Republican Ronald Reagan, which Ford narrowly won, then the national presidential election against Democrat Jimmy Carter, which Ford lost.

Ford died on December 26, 2006, having lived ninety-three years and 165 days, making him the oldest surviving US president.

THANKSGIVING DINNER

{ The foods on the table at today's Thanksgiving dinner
are pretty much the same as those served at the first
such feast in 1621 which celebrated the successful
initial harvest at the Plimoth (modern Plymouth)
Plantation. The menu has become traditional and the
foods served emblematic of this holiday.
Don't you believe it. }

The customary Thanksgiving dinner now features roast turkey,
accompanied by mashed potatoes, usually with gravy, stuffing,
sweet potato pie, sweet corn, cranberry sauce, and various fall
vegetables (generally some form of squash), all followed by
pumpkin or apple pie. But this conventional menu is not likely
the same as that served in 1621. Only one written record of that
dinner exists, and it is incomplete, mentioning only deer and
wildfowl. But many of these other dishes would not have graced
the table in 1621 simply because they weren't available.

Historical authorities tend to think that rather than turkey,
the fowl served was more likely goose or duck, or maybe even
swan. Potatoes hadn't yet reached North America, bread stuffing
would have been unknown, corn would have been served off the
cob as porridge, cranberries would not have been made into sauce
since sugar was sparse, and pumpkins and apples would not have
been converted into pie because the Plantation had neither butter
nor wheat flour to make the pie crust. Besides, the colony had no
oven for baking.

Furthermore, food historians are fairly certain that unlike
today's Thanksgiving menus, seafood was a staple of the dinner—
mussels and clams were plentiful nearby, as were lobster and bass.
Attendee Edward Winslow wrote that the feast extended over a
three-day period and was attended by the fifty surviving pilgrims
and "some 90" of the Wampanoag natives.

CHOPIN'S MINUTE WALTZ

{
One of Chopin's most memorable pieces is this popular short piano waltz meant to be played in sixty seconds, thus the name.
Don't you believe it.
}

That name, as usually read, is a misinterpretation. To be truer to Chopin's intention, the word "minute" should be pronounced with the stress on the second syllable, thus meaning very small, as in miniature waltz. Its tempo is stipulated as *molto vivace*, meaning very lively, but the composer did not design this piece—captioned as *Waltz in D-flat major, Opus 64, No. 1*—to be completed in one minute, although some pianists rush through it trying to perform it in that interval. It was created as a small piece, not a rapid one, meant to be played in about one and one-half to two minutes; in concert its performance usually takes just about two minutes. The waltz is 140 measures long; playing it in one minute would be quite a feat.

It is said that Chopin was inspired to write this 1847 piece in by watching a little dog chase its tail, and he named it *Valse du petit chien*, "Waltz of the small dog." It is one of Chopin's better known musical pieces and is performed frequently in concert, easily available, as are most of his compositions, because it is written for piano and does not require the presence of a large orchestra. The typical elegance of Chopin's music displays why he is frequently referred to as "the poet of the piano."

With lyrics by Lan O'Kun, a vocal version was recorded by Barbra Streisand on her 1966 album, *Call Me Barbra*. The lyrics reinforce the idea that the song should be performed in one minute, although Streisand's version runs close to two minutes.

SPINACH

{
The cartoon character Popeye gained his strength from eating spinach because spinach is loaded with power-generating iron.
Don't you believe it.
}

Popeye, a cartoon sailorman who first appeared in the 1929 comic strip *Thimble Theatre*, attributed his excessive strength to the virtues of spinach. Whenever he faced a situation that required his special talents, he would break open a can of spinach and slurp it down. His muscles would swell along with his determination. But was this a misconception? Spinach contains a fair amount of iron, but nowhere near as much as the nutritionists' chart had displayed.

The misunderstanding dates back to 1870 when a German chemist named Erich von Wolf was researching the amount of iron in spinach and other green vegetables. When tabulating his findings, he mistakenly entered a decimal point in the wrong place, making the recorded iron content in spinach ten times as much as he actually measured. Mr. Wolf found that the amount of iron in spinach was 3.5 milligrams in a 100-gram serving, but he mistakenly recorded 35 milligrams. This then became the accepted measurement which found its way into nutrition tables around the world, and the mishap became fact.

When the Popeye cartoon was being devised, his creators—having read about the fallacious superabundance of iron in spinach—decided to make that vegetable the source of his strength. His observation that he is "strong to the finish, 'cause I eats my spinach," though it sounds good, is rooted in the transcription error made decades earlier. By the time the mistake was discovered in 1937 it was too late to alter the strip. Popeye had been getting his strength from spinach for almost ten years.

And the myth has lived on. Even an article in the *British Medical Journal* in 1981, meant to finally correct the error, has not changed the public's perception.

AMERICANS FIGHTING RUSSIANS

{ Although the United States and the Soviets faced off against one another during the Cold War, American forces have never actually fought the Russians. **Don't you believe it.** }

Actually, they did. But it wasn't during the Cold War. History seems to have forgotten the "undeclared war" between the United States and Russia from 1918–20.

America entered World War I in April 1917, its troops arriving in France on June 26. In Russia, the February Revolution had just deposed the Tsar and installed a provisional government eventually led by Alexander Kerensky, who pledged to continue fighting the Germans on the Eastern Front. But the Imperial Russian Army suffered a devastating loss in June. The Kerensky government was then overthrown by the Bolsheviks in the October Revolution. In March 1918 the new Bolshevik government signed the Treaty of Brest-Litvosk with the Central Powers and withdrew from the war.

But the United States, in support of Kerensky, had sent Russia military supplies worth millions of dollars, which were now piled up at the Russian ports of Vladivostok, Murmansk, and Arkhangelsk, and in jeopardy of seizure by the Germans or Bolsheviks. Another problem was how to help the 40,000 Czech prisoners due for repatriation now that Russia had left the war. The Bolsheviks offered these prisoners free passage to France so they could join the Allies on the Western Front. But hostilities erupted between the Czech Legion and the Bolsheviks in May 1918 and the Czechs were stranded in Northern Russia.

The British and French felt the Bolsheviks were a threat to their influence in the area and also to other countries if the communist bug began to infect other European peoples. They thus decided to help White Russian anti-Bolsheviks resist the revolutionary Russian Reds. Short of available troops, they convinced President Wilson that sending American forces was in America's greatest self-interest. In August 1918, though still fighting in Western Europe, American soldiers were dispatched to Russia in two separate operations.

About 5,000 troops, the "Polar Bear Expedition," were moved to Arkhangelsk, 600 miles north of Moscow, on a threefold mission: to protect war supplies formerly sent to the Russian army, to aid in the evacuation of the Czech Legion which was stranded along the Trans-Siberian Railroad, and to fight the Bolsheviks in order to persuade Russia to resurrect the Eastern Front against Germany. A show of strength in the area was also meant to dissuade the Germans from opening a new theatre of operations. Allied forces engaged in a number of skirmishes against the Bolsheviks, and won more than they lost.

The other detachment, the American Expeditionary Force Siberia, consisted of 8,000 troops sent to Vladivostok to protect the Trans-Siberian Railway. They were again sent to safeguard war materiel and rolling stock that had been provided to the White Russian army, which included several hundred locomotives and several thousand railway cars, and to protect the locals from Cossack forays. This was an international force, in addition to French and various British colonials the largest contingents were Czech, Greek, Estonian, Japanese, and American. The winter was dismal with Siberian temperatures frequently hitting sixty below. American forces mainly fought the frigid climate, the Cossacks, and Bolshevik Partisans, but rarely against communist soldiers.

Troops from Archangelsk were withdrawn in early 1919, the last American soldiers left Siberia on April 1, 1920. Soon after the US troops were withdrawn from Russia, President Warren G. Harding called the expedition a mistake and, ever the politician, blamed the previous administration.

A BURNING RIVER

{ Water is used to extinguish fires because it doesn't burn.
Don't you believe it. }

This is generally a true statement, but not always. In June 1969, the Cuyahoga River in northeastern Ohio actually caught fire, burning two railway bridges. For years recognized as one of the most polluted rivers in the United States, its decades-old, inherited industrial waste included accumulated oil that produced the river's flammability. In covering the fire, *Time* magazine described the river as one that "oozes rather than flows," in which a person "does not drown but decays."

The river had a history of pollution fires, thirteen in the previous century, the largest in 1952, which caused a million dollars in damage to boats and structures. For decades the residents of Cleveland had quietly ignored the degradation of their river, accepting its contamination as the price they had to pay for industrial prosperity of their city. They even recognized that the section of river from Cleveland to Akron was devoid of fish. But by 1969, the attitude toward pollution was changing, both the government and its citizens becoming aware that fouling the environment was more than a short-term problem. The 1969 fire contributed to the positive change that was already happening.

Awakening to the new environmentalism, in the previous year Cleveland had passed a one million dollar bond undertaking the clean-up of the Cuyahoga River. But the fire helped focus national interest on pollution control. It also served as a stimulus for the founding of the Environmental Protection Agency in 1970 and the federal Clean Water Act of 1972.

Water quality of the river improved over the following years, aided by the economic downturn of the late seventies that closed many of Cleveland's polluting factories.

ENDING THE CIVIL WAR

The Civil War ended on April 9, 1965, when Confederate General Lee surrendered to Union General Grant at the Appomattox Court House in Virginia. **Don't you believe it.**

The war didn't end then. Lee surrendered only the Army of Northern Virginia; other branches remained in the field for various periods through the following eleven weeks. Confederate commanders were left on their own to surrender to Union officers.

Various units capitulated throughout the spring. The first, some six hours after Lee, was General St. John Richardson Liddell and the infantry at Mobile. The last was General Stand Watie, the only Native American general during the Civil War, commander of the Indian Cavalry Brigade, on June 23, 1865.

But that still wasn't the end. When Lee surrendered, the Confederate ship *Shenandoah* was in the Bering Sea, preying on Union whalers. The *Shenandoah* was not a warship and never fought against Union vessels. Her quarry were unarmed merchant ships, especially the New Bedford whaling fleet which supplied the Union with military materiel, smokeless lamp fuel, and lubricating oil.

The ship's captain, Lieutenant Commander James Waddell, didn't learn of Lee's surrender until late in June. Waddell wished to surrender his ship, but chose a European port because at a Union port he might be tried for piracy and his entire crew hanged. A good decision, because he learned later that commerce raiders were not given the same amnesty as Confederate soldiers.

The final Confederate surrender took place in Liverpool, England, on November 6, 1865, when the CSS *Shenandoah* lowered her flag for the last time.

On August 20, 1866, President Johnson finally declared an end to the war, some sixteen months after Appomattox.

THE FIRST NOVEL

{ *Don Quixote* is considered one of the most influential
novels of all time, but is it the first of it genre?
Don't you believe it. }

Don Quixote has been recognized the first modern novel, but
literary authorities pretty well agree that the first fully achieved
novel was *The Tale of Genji*, an eleventh-century Japanese work
written by a noblewoman named Murasaki Shikibu. Recognized
as a classic, *The Tale of Genji* displayed the characteristics that
came to define the novel format: it is a fictional narrative that
describes intimate human experience, with psychological observation and characters that develop over time.

The Tale of Genji hosts a cast of over 400 characters, but it
focuses on Hikaru Genji, son of the medieval Japanese emperor,
and his romantic affairs. In fifty-four loosely connected chapters,
it depicts a wide range of courtiers and their diverse lifestyles,
among them his amours and his relationships with them.

Characters are delineated in a variety of cutting portraits,
some tragic, some humiliating, some hilarious.

Perhaps the reason that *The Tale of Genji* is not as widely-read
as *Don Quixote* is the difficulty it presents to the modern reader;
despite the substantial number of dramatis personae almost none
are given an explicit name. Instead, they are identified by their
role, their title, or their relation to other characters, which often
changes as the story advances. Many readers assign nicknames to
the many characters in order to keep tabs on them.

Partial translations into English appeared in 1882 (by
Kenchō) and the 1920s (by Waley), but it wasn't until 1976 that
Edward Seidensticker published an English version of the full
novel.

Franklin Pierce Re-nomination

> The presidency, the highest office in the land, is a prize for any political party. Should an elected president run for a second term, he is of course guaranteed the re-nomination of his party.
> **Don't you believe it.**

There was one occasion when a sitting president was denied his party's support for a re-election. The year was 1856 and the president was Democrat Franklin Pierce. Four years earlier, Pierce had been nominated as the Democratic candidate for president on the forty-ninth ballot at the 1852 Democratic National Convention. With his running mate, William R. King, he easily defeated the Whig ticket of Winfield Scott and William A. Graham, taking 86 percent of the electoral vote.

But Pierce's presidency was marked by increased tension between northern and southern interests. The polarization was further aggravated by passage of the 1854 Kansas-Nebraska Act, which was intended to resolve the issue of slavery expanding into the territories. Applying the principle of "popular sovereignty," it asserted that the settlers in each territory—not Congress—should decide for themselves whether or not to adopt slavery. But despite its best intentions, it failed pitifully, having the opposite effect of inducing violence between pro- and anti-slavery blocs in Kansas.

The Kansas-Nebraska Act turned out to be one of the key political transactions that led to the Civil War. Further, it deepened the wedge between factions of the Democratic Party. Northern Democrats, fearing extension of slavery, were uneasy with the Act; Southern Democrats generally welcomed it. The bill also amplified anti-slavery inclinations in the North, which contributed to the founding of the Republican Party.

In such a climate, the idea of re-electing Pierce did not capture much positive sentiment in Democratic backrooms.

MAGNA CARTA

{
The Magna Carta, one of the most famous documents
in world history, defined a whole new catalog of rights
for the English people when it was signed.
Don't you believe it.
}

The Magna Carta, executed in June 1215 at Runnymede, near
Windsor, is seen by many English citizens as "the fountain of our
liberty." But actually, it didn't deal with the rights of ordinary
people at all; it was intended rather as a détente between King
John and the English barons. Even so, the Magna Carta still
didn't satisfy its purpose. Mutual antipathy was not diminished
between the king and his barons; rather, it became more intense.
By September of that year the barons had organized their opposition to the king while he successfully appealed to the Vatican to
have the Magna Carta revoked.

The long-lived myth of the Magna Carta states that it
protected personal liberties for English citizens. But it didn't. It
did, however, provide a foundation for some basic legal notions,
such as the right to trial by one's peers and a ban on cruel and
unusual punishments.

Additionally, the Magna Carta is not really a unique document.
Previous monarchs had issued charters on assuming the throne.
In 1100, Henry I had produced a coronation charter in which he
assured he would govern fairly, end the royal intrusion into the
family affairs of the barons, and allow the clergy increased financial
autonomy. Henry of course did not adhere to his guarantees, but his
charter did provide the basis for the agreement of 1215.

Later kings whittled down the document from its original
sixty-nine clauses, repealing obsolete laws, until the mid-twen-
tieth century when only three remained: one granting freedom to
the Church of England, a second prohibiting arbitrary arrest and
the sale of justice, and the third preserving the liberties of the city
of London.

Still not much for individual rights.

STILL MORE QUICK ONES

It is erroneously believed that Sitting Bull killed Lt. Col. George Armstrong Custer in the battle of the Little Bighorn on June 25, 1876. Not possible. Sitting Bull wasn't even in the battle. But he did serve as his tribe's holy man. His earlier premonitions that all his enemies would be delivered to him was fulfilled by Custer's Last Stand.

Chinese checkers did not originate in China, and the game doesn't use checkers. The game is of German origin (named "Sternhalma"), and it is played with marbles on a hexagram-shaped board by two to six players. It was popular in the United States and even in Japan before the Chinese even heard of it.

Chalk, the kind used to write on blackboards, is not chalk. It is really calcined gypsum, more popularly known as plaster of Paris.

Bill Gates, the founder of the Microsoft Corporation, inventor of Microsoft software, and the richest man in the world for six consecutive years, never finished college.

The United States is not composed of fifty states. Technically, there are only forty-six states. Kentucky, Massachusetts, Pennsylvania, and Virginia are commonwealths.

The financial crash of 1929 did not generate a spate of jumpers. Only two are confirmed, one a clerk who had worked for a brokerage for over twenty-five years, the other a businessman who leapt from his broker's window. But there is no record of either brokers or bankers jumping out of windows.

THE REVOLUTION'S FIRST CASUALTY

{ Given the paucity of news services during the Revolutionary War, it is no surprise that our records from the period somehow did not popularize the name of the first colonist to be killed in confrontation with British troops.
Don't you believe it. }

We do know his name. It's Crispus Attucks, and he was an African-American seaman, the first of five men killed at the Boston Massacre on March 5, 1770 and thus the first casualty of the American Revolution.

We know little of Attucks's early years or family life, only that his father was a slave who had been shipped here from Africa and his mother a Natick Indian. Born into slavery, Attucks had run away from his master in Framingham, Massachusetts. An advertisement seeking his return, described him as "A Molatto Fellow, about 27 Years of age . . . 6 Feet two Inches high, short curl'd Hair," and offered ten dollars for his return. Attucks spent the next two decades serving on ships out of Boston Harbor, and working as a ropemaker. He seemed unafraid of being captured and returned to slave status, but now he faced a different danger—as the relations between the Americans and the British deteriorated and the Royal Navy starting to run short of naval personnel, seamen were always in jeopardy of being impressed into the British Navy.

On this particular day, Attucks was involved in an encounter that went from verbal jousting to physical violence. The details of the confrontation are not clear, but it is known that a group of Bostonians were taunting a British soldier when a squad of British redcoats appeared to support their comrades. Soon more Bostonians joined in, then more redcoats, and shots rang out; Attucks was the first colonial to be killed.

THE TELEPHONE

{
The telephone was invented by Alexander Graham Bell.
Don't you believe it.
}

On March 10, 1876, Bell used his rudimentary telephone to call his assistant Thomas Watson in the next room, "Mr. Watson," he is reputed to have said, "Come here. I want to see you." But that's only part of the story.

Antonio Santi Giuseppe Meucci, an Italian immigrant to the United States, began working on the design of a *telegrafo parlante* (talking telegraph) in 1849. When his wife became paralyzed in 1855 he devised a contrivance to link her bedroom with his nearby workshop, and in 1860 held a public demonstration. But he couldn't afford to file a patent.

Later improving his communication system, Meucci filed a one-year renewable patent caveat in 1871. However, facing financial hardship due to his wife's illness and lacking sufficient English-language skills to function in the business world, Meucci could not renew his caveat and it expired.

In his last attempt to secure backing, he sent a model and drawings to the American District Telegraph Co.; they later said they had misplaced his exhibits. But after two years they turned up in the hands of the man who shared Meucci's lab and who secured a US patent in March 1876. That man was Alexander Bell.

Meucci sued Bell in January 1887. Bell's patent came into question and a move to annul the patent was issued on the grounds of fraud and misrepresentation. However, Meucci died in October 1889 and the case was subsequently discontinued.

But 113 years later, on June 11, 2002, Meucci finally won his case when the US House of Representatives acknowledged him as the true inventor of the telephone. The declaration was barely noticed in the States. But it was greeted by celebrations in his home town of Florence, Italy.

Meucci died penniless and is still virtually unknown in the United States.

G.I.

{
"G.I." was devised in military parlance to mean "Government Issue," designating any item furnished by the government for the armed forces.
Don't you believe it.
}

Actually, the military originally used the abbreviation G.I. to mean "galvanized iron," a category in US Army inventories that included such items as metal trash cans. Later, during World War I, G.I. was wrongly interpreted as "Government Issue," or "General Issue," for the many items of equipment supplied for military application. By extension, as a noun, it also was used to mean a member or a veteran of the US armed forces.

The term came into popular use with the advent of the Selective Service Draft in 1940, with its application expanding throughout the World War II. In those years G.I. Joe became the familiar name for any man in the uniform of any branch of the military, but mostly the army or air force. Servicemen also referred to themselves derisively as "G.I.," by which they meant General Issue, implying that they were just another class of items that were as disposable as their boots, belts, canteens, helmets, or Jeeps.

It should be noted that "G.I." is also used as a verb in military parlance, describing the extreme cleaning of a location or an item to an excessive level of immaculacy. Soldiers are ordered to G.I. an area when a senior officer is expected to perform an inspection.

The initialing, of course, has different meanings in different contexts. In medicine, for example, it means "gastrointestinal"; in food science "glycemic index"; in fiber optics "graded index"; in atmospheric sciences "Geophysical Institute"; in social media messages "great idea."

But in military applications it implies something (or somebody) provided by and totally in the control of the government.

THREE BRASS BALLS

{
The three brass balls hanging in front of a pawnshop signify the odds of two to one that you'll never retrieve your possessions.
Don't you believe it.
}

It's an old joke, but not likely the truth, obviously. Then where does the symbol come from?

Actually, the agglomerated three brass balls derive from Italian nobility, and are the emblem of the Medici family of Lombardy. The Medicis, believed to be financial representatives of the Papacy, introduced the profession of money lending to England. To mark their place of business, they displayed their family crest—three brass balls—in front of their residence.

And, as with any profitable venture, others soon entered money-lending in competition, keeping the then well-known three brass balls as the trade's trademark.

But this history still begs the question of how the Medici clan happened to adopt that symbol as their family crest. One explanation is that the name Medici can be traced to the practice of medicine, and that several early family members were physicians for whom a pill was the profession's trademark. But, though a pill is round, why three?

Another theory tells of Averardo de' Medici, a military comrade of Charlemagne, who became famous for slaying the giant Mugello. As the story goes, after the combat Averardo acquired the giant's club which was ornamented with three iron balls that he later adopted as his own emblem.

Still another theory shuns any reference to the Medicis and relates the triad to the indicant of Nicholas of Bari, a fourth-century saint, who is reputed have given bags of gold to a poor man's three daughters so they could each possess a dowry and be able to marry.

As with many of today's images, the roots we seek are at best speculative, dating too far back to trace, but nonetheless have become ubiquitous.

THREE VOLLEYS OVER A GRAVE

{ The three rounds of shots fired over a soldier's grave symbolize the three periods of his life—the before-life, the life as lived, and the afterlife.
Don't you believe it. }

It was once believed that the deceased must be sheltered from evil spirits because satanic demons attached themselves to the dead and only loud noises could scare them away. The louder the noise, the more effective the deterrent, or so went the belief. The same explanation would apply to the ringing of bells accompanying a funeral.

At the intersection of superstition and warfare, it became apparent that the noise most appropriate for deceased military personnel would, of course, be gunshots. The explosive sounds of gunfire are familiar to warriors, being an accompaniment to their very lives, and would therefore be the proper send-off to their Valhalla. It would be fitting end, indicating that the honoree had fallen in battle (whether actually or metaphorically), and was dutiful to the last. The tradition of signaling with gunshots comes from an old custom on the battlefield, where three volleys indicated the end of a temporary ceasefire that had been called to clear the dead. They further indicated that the dead had been removed from the field and fighting could be resumed.

But why specifically three volleys? Enter belief in the Holy Trinity. As a child, the soldier would have been baptized in the name of the Father, the Son, and the Holy Ghost. Now, at the other end of his life, he is ushered into the next world with the same three attending, this time not denoted in words but symbolized in the currency of his military service—gunfire. Accompanied by the reverential declaration, "Earth to earth, ashes to ashes, dust to dust."

AL CAPONE'S FALL

Al Capone, known as "Scarface," headed the Chicago mafia during the Prohibition era, and was the best-known criminal of his day. He was finally brought down by a fearless, incorruptible FBI agent named Elliot Ness.
Don't you believe it.

Capone was put out of business not by heavy hitter Ness, but by a mild-mannered accountant named Frank J. Wilson.

Elliot Ness did manage to do severe damage to Capone's operations, but he was not the one who accumulated the damning evidence that led to Capone's conviction. For three years, under supervision of Treasury Department accountant Frank J. Wilson and aided by US Attorney George E. Q. Johnson, investigators collected countless examples of income tax law violations prompted by a 1927 Supreme Court ruling that any income from criminal activities must be subjected to income taxes.

Capone's criminal activities centered on bootlegging, but his illegal empire also reached into gambling, prostitution, racketeering, and other illegitimate practices. Notorious for both his ruthlessness and his organizational skills, Capone governed his empire by bribing the police and politicians and by menacing witnesses.

Capone had successfully defended against several accusations of racketeering, but could not so easily escape charges of violating the tax law. On October 17, 1931, he was found guilty of five counts of tax evasion, two of which were felonies. He had also been accused of 5,000 violations of the Volstead Act, but these were dropped in favor of the tax charges. He was sentenced to eleven years in prison. Following a failed appeal, Capone began his jail time in 1932.

After seven years in prison Capone was released in 1939, his mind devastated by syphilis. He died in 1947. Wilson went on to become Chief of the United States Secret Service.

GRAHAM CRACKERS

{
The graham cracker was created so that kids could enjoy s'mores.
Don't you believe it.
}

The graham cracker was invented as part of an ostensible health program conceived in 1829 by Reverend Sylvester Graham, a Presbyterian minister in New Jersey. Graham was alarmed by the use of only white flour in baked goods to the disregard of nutrients in the rest of the grain. He saw refined white flour as a source of carnal urges that produced a whole catalog of sins and maladies.

As a healthy alternative he created graham flour, which when baked becomes the graham cracker. It was perceived as a primary constituent of a pure food diet that could suppress sexual desire and thus promote a healthier lifestyle. He believed that eating the right foods would serve to curb a person's sexual appetite. This was a belief, incidentally, shared by John Kellogg, of cornflakes fame.

Graham flour is made by separating the endosperm of the wheat kernel from the bran and germ. The endosperm is then finely ground while the bran and germ are coarsely ground separately. When recombined, the result is a coarse-textured flour that produces crackers with distinctive taste and texture, and believed to be highly salubrious.

While the original graham crackers were only slightly or not-at-all sweetened, today's descendants are more commonly laden with sugar or honey, making them more akin to cookies than to crackers. Many commercial "graham crackers" now use more white flour than graham flour and are may be adorned with cinnamon or chocolate, no longer qualifying them as a health food.

But they still make tasty s'mores!

TO THE BACK OF THE BUS

> Named "the first lady of civil rights" by Congress, Rosa Parks, a young black civil rights activist, in December 1955 refused to give up her white-only seat and move to the colored section of a bus in Montgomery, Alabama, setting off the movement to desegregate public transportation.
> **Don't you believe it.**

Others had resisted bus segregation—notably Bayard Rustin in 1942 and Sarah Louise Keys in 1952—but the first such recorded incident occurred in New York City ninety years before Rosa Parks. On Sunday, July 16, 1854, a twenty-four-year-old free-born, black schoolteacher named Elizabeth Jennings, late for church where she was an organist, did not notice the restrictive sign on the arriving trolley and boarded the conveyance intended for whites only.

At the time, public transportation consisted of horse-drawn streetcars owned by private companies that enforced segregated seating and gave the conductor the right to deny service to any passenger. When she refused to get off the trolley the conductor and a local policeman forcibly ejected her and dumped her on the sidewalk.

But Elizabeth Jennings was from an influential family of New York's black community, linked with black abolition ministers, journalists, educators, and businessmen; she brought suit, and was represented by Chester A. Arthur (later our twenty-first president) against the trolley conductor and the Third Avenue Railroad Company. She won the case, receiving a small cash award and a court order to the company to allow blacks on their trolleys.

Still, Rosa Parks is better known than Elizabeth Jennings, largely because segregation was in the public consciousness in the 1950s and news was disseminated widely via television and other media.

But Elizabeth Jennings was there first.

CRUCIFIXION

{ Crucifixion was rarely used as punishment before Jesus.
Don't you believe it. }

Crucifixion had been around for at least 500 years before Christ. According to the *Encyclopedia Britannica*, the first historical record of crucifixion dates to about 519 BC when "Darius I, king of Persia, crucified 3,000 political opponents in Babylon." It was practiced by the Carthaginians and and is mentioned in the Qur'an as a form of punishment.

Crucifixion is a method of execution in which the condemned is tied or nailed to a beam and left to hang free until death occurs. The method results in a slow and painful death from any one or a combination of several causes: cardiac rupture, heart failure, acidosis, hypovolemic shock, asphyxia, arrhythmia, and pulmonary embolism. The most common cause is asphyxiation—when the total body weight is supported by outstretched arms, the lungs collapse because the contorted position of the hanging body prevents inhalation.

Execution by crucifixion also has social implications. It is a humiliating way to die, a dishonorable death. In Rome, it was inflicted only on those of low social status—slaves, pirates, gladiators, and enemies of the state. Citizens of Roman society were rarely subject to any capital punishment; instead they were fined or exiled. The only exception for Roman citizens was as punishment for major crimes against the state, such as treason.

In any case, it was abolished in the Roman Empire by Constantine the Great, the first Christian emperor, early in the fourth century as an expression of reverence for Jesus. But its emblem lives on as a symbol of Christianity.

GEORGE M. COHAN

{
Considered by many as "the father of musical comedy," multitalented George M. Cohan presented himself to his audiences as the Yankee Doodle boy and delighted in revealing that he was born on the Fourth of July. **Don't you believe it.**
}

Songwriter, playwright, singer, dancer, actor, and producer, George M. Cohan dominated musical theatre in the decade before World War I. He wrote, produced, and starred in some three dozen Broadway musicals and composed over 300 songs, among the most memorable being "Give My Regards to Broadway." He referred to himself "just a song and dance man," but during his career he starred in vaudeville, musical comedy, drama, on screen, and on radio.

As a child, Cohan traveled with a family act, appearing with his sister and parents as the Four Cohans. A show-business veteran before he was ten, by thirteen he was touring in the title role as the star of *Peck's Bad Boy*. He went on to become the leading light in American musical theater of the time. In 1936 President Franklin Delano Roosevelt awarded him the Congressional Gold Medal for his contributions to World War I morale, especially the songs "You're a Grand Old Flag" and "Over There."

A headliner until his retirement, Cohan is memorialized by a statue in Times Square in New York City commemorating his contributions to American musical theater. On his death President Roosevelt said of him, "He will be mourned by millions whose lives were brightened and whose burdens were eased by his genius as a fun maker and as a dispeller of gloom."

But Cohan, though widely praised and fondly remembered, was not born on July 4th. His baptismal certificate affirms that he was born in Providence, Rhode Island, on July 3, 1878.

BLITZED LONDONERS

{
Film clips from England during the blitz confirm that
Londoners took the nightly bombing in good spirits
and never lost their social cohesion.
Don't you believe it.
}

Every movie set in London during the Second World War has
the compulsory bombing scene in which convivial locals parade
en masse into the underground rail stations carrying flagons of
ale and singing "Roll out the barrel." It's a nice scene, affirming
the Brits' resolute tenacity. But it's not totally accurate. People
were more discontent.

Beginning on September 7, 1940, London was bombed by
the Luftwaffe for fifty-seven consecutive nights. Londoners held
up well under the bombings. They tended their homes, went to
their jobs, cared for their children, and generally did what residents do, as much as that was possible under wartime conditions.
But citizens were not all that complaisant, especially after dark
when they migrated underground for the night. The king and
queen left the city every night for the relative safety of Windsor,
but the general populace had no escape from the bombs.

With blacked-out streets and a police force diminished
by military enlistments, criminal activity mushroomed. Break-
ins, thefts, holdups, pickpocketing, burglaries, and looting all
increased dramatically. One observer reckoned that shopkeepers
lost more from crime than they did from German bombs. Prostitution flourished. And many otherwise righteous citizens fell into
antisocial activity: stealing clothing and petrol coupons, dealing in
the black market, stripping valuables from victims in the streets.

Although the stress of the war led some to anxiety attacks,
fatigue, eating disorders, sleep disturbance, miscarriages, and other
physical and mental ailments, morale didn't disintegrate.

But the proverbial stiff upper lip did quiver a bit.

POPE GREGORY AND THE BLACK DEATH

{ The policies of Pope Gregory IX increased the severity of the Black Death. **You can believe it.** }

Gregory IX, Pope from March 1227 until August 1241, was born Ugolino di Conti, the nephew of Pope Innocent III. He is known for instituting the Papal Inquisition, an agency for severely punishing heretics, which established procedures that became the basis for the uglier Inquisition three centuries later. He is also known as a principal proponent of Church teaching that discriminated against Jews and condemned them to an inferior status in Christendom.

But his most destructive pronouncement came in his papal bull, *Vox in Rama*, which condemned a German heresy known as Luciferian, and described the practices of the sect that followed a form of adoration worshiping both the devil and a diabolical black cat. It portrayed the cat as an incarnation of Satan, leading to the mass elimination of cats. The decline in the cat population caused an increase in the rat population. And since rats were the hosts for the fleas that carried disease, as the rats grew in number so did the fleas, which accelerated the spread of the plague.

Research reveals that the "Great Pestilence" began in Central Asia early in the fourteenth century and spread west, ravaging large pieces of Asia, Asia Minor, and the Middle East before hitting Europe. It followed trade routes and traveled mostly by ship. When it took hold in Europe, the Black Death destroyed close to half the population, estimated at over fifty million people.

Felinophobia persisted in Europe until the early nineteenth century. There is still a comparative shortage of black cats in Europe to this day, excluding the British Isles.

And all because of belief in witchery and Satanism.

MUTINY ON THE *BOUNTY*

{ As told in five different films made over the course of seventy years, the story of the 1789 mutiny on the ship *Bounty* tells how Royal Navy Lieutenant William Bligh provoked his seamen to revolt by his sadistic management of his crew.
Don't you believe it. }

Most of the films got it wrong. Bligh's problem was not sadism but leniency in commanding his crew.

Consider the fictional Bligh: The earliest film, *The Mutiny of the Bounty*, was an Australian-New Zealand silent made in 1916, the only version not to demonize Bligh and reputedly the most historically accurate of all. No prints have survived.

The later ones, with sound, were released in 1933, 1935, 1962, and 1984, respectively, all portraying Bligh as a monster, inflating the drama at the expense of accuracy. The best-known known is the 1935 film, with Charles Laughton as Bligh and Clark Gable as Fletcher Christian, Bligh's first mate.

The problem with these films is their depiction of Bligh as a tormenting martinet, whereas in truth, he was a disciplinarian but one not unconcerned about his crew's health and living conditions. Yet he gradually lost authority by limiting the punishment for his men's transgressions.

Bligh, at thirty-three, had extensive seagoing experience, both in the Royal Navy and the merchant service. First going to sea at age six as a cabin boy, by age twenty-two he had been appointed sailing master of the *Resolution*, captained by James Cook in his final and fatal voyage. Christian had previously sailed with Bligh twice, under his tutelage becoming a skilled navigator. When Bligh took command of the *Bounty*, he chose Christian as his master's mate. Christian frequently dined with Bligh on shipboard.

The voyage to Tahiti was intended to secure breadfruit plants and transport them to England's Caribbean colonies to be used as foodstuff for slaves. But the mission was low on the Admiralty's priorities. His assigned ship was too small and the available space for its intended cargo was too limiting, lacking provision for the other commissioned officers and marine detachment befitting the captain of such a long voyage. He was not conferred the status "master and commander," nor was he advanced in rank, leading the voyage as a lieutenant.

The *Bounty* left England in December 1877, reached Tahiti in October 1788, and tied up for over five months while loading its cargo. On Tahiti, the crew found contentment, many living ashore—the climate was pleasant, the duty unexacting, the Tahitians hospitable, their women acquiescent. But the soft life proved harmful to discipline. Overt discord between Bligh and his crew started to develop.

On April 4, 1789, the *Bounty* departed Tahiti with its cargo of more than 1,000 breadfruit saplings. Three weeks later, at sea, Christian and twenty-five crewmen seized the ship. The reason who for the mutiny has never been fully exposed, but likely partly a reaction to leaving the easy living and sexual freedom of Tahiti to return to the drudgery of ordinary seamen. Rather than execute Bligh, the mutineers set him adrift in an open twenty-three-foot-long boat along with those seamen who remained loyal, thereby, they thought, consigning him to the mercy of the sea. However, Bligh and his men, in a remarkable show of seamanship, supported by only a quadrant and a compass, managed to navigate some 3,600 miles and reach the East Indies in mid-June.

Back in England, Bligh was court-martialed, a routine review when a captain loses his ship, and was found innocent of wrongdoing. A year later, he was assigned a new ship and sent again for breadfruit, this time on a full-size ship with a full complement of officers and marines. Bligh later penned a memoir, *Narrative of the Mutiny*, which said little about the uprising but concentrated on his small-boat voyage. The mutineers settled on an uncharted island and burned their ship so they could never return.

THE CROISSANT

{ The croissant is one of those delicious delicacies deftly devised by the French.
Don't you believe it. }

Nothing is more stereotypically Parisian than sitting at an outdoor table on the Champs-Élysées enjoying *un tasse de café-au-lait* along with a fresh croissant. But contrary to popular belief, the croissant wasn't born in France. Rather, it traces its origin to Austria, where it was designed as a celebratory treat honoring the liberation of the Austrian empire from the Muslim Turks.

The most popular legend about the origin of the croissant is set in 1683 Vienna, when the city was undergoing a siege by Ottoman Turks. The tale tells of bakers who were working late one night when they heard rumblings underground. The Turks, unable to breach the city's walls, had taken instead to tunneling underneath them. The bakers informed the city's defenders who destroyed the tunnels and thus saved the city and the empire. In celebration of the victory over the Turks, the bakers fashioned a pastry in the shape of the crescents they had seen on the enemy's battle flags, the crescent being the symbol of Islam. They called it *kipferl*, German for crescent.

A hundred years later, when Princess Marie Antoinette married King Louis XVI of France, the bakers in Paris, to honor the new Queen, made a version of *kipferl* for her, which they named croissant. From that point, the Viennese pastry took on a decidedly French character, often filled with chocolate, raisins, jam, or cheese, sometimes even with meat.

Another legend traces the croissant to the late 1830s when an Austrian bakery opened on the rue de Richelieu in Paris. Among its Viennese specialties was *kipferl*, which inspired imitation by the local *boulangeries*, which, of course, renamed it in French.

In any case, it is originally Viennese, not French.

THE WORST RIGID AIRSHIP DISASTER

As early as the late 1800s, rigid airships were being considered as potential carriers for long distance travel. But they proved to be too frangible to fulfill their promise, especially when the *Hindenburg* burned in May 1937.

Don't you believe it.

Though better remembered, the *Hindenburg* accident was not the first nor the most disastrous to befall airships. Four years earlier, in April 1933, the USS *Akron* went down with a loss of life almost double that of the *Hindenburg*. The *Akron* was a 6,500,000-cubic foot rigid airship supported by inert helium, which was safer than the *Hindenburg*'s combustible hydrogen. It was commissioned in October 1931, intended as a flying aircraft carrier for several fighter planes that could be launched and recovered while she was in flight.

The *Akron* was used in research, exploring the capabilities of the rigid airship as a weapon system. It was tested by the Navy as scouting and observation support for the fleet. For the remainder of 1931 and 1932, the *Akron* served and expanded its capabilities primarily on both the east and west coasts but also elsewhere in the United States. It served in Florida to explore sites for naval bases in the Navy's southern zone, and then over Cuba and Panama.

While stationed in the New England area, Akron encountered a severe storm flying over the New Jersey coast and, early on the morning of April 4, 1933, crashed into the sea. Of the seventy-six men on board only three survived. Another Navy craft, a non-rigid airship, also crashed while searching for possible survivors, killing two more men.

This accident produced the greatest loss of life in any known airship crash.

THE ALAMO

{ The two hundred men who fought for the Alamo bravely defended a piece of America from the horde of Mexicans intent on usurping it.
Don't you believe it. }

The defenders of the Alamo certainly were brave. But their legitimacy was not at all so indisputable. The Alamo, a retired mission built early in the eighteenth century and secularized in 1793, was on Mexican soil. The men who fought for it were as much insurgents as defenders.

Beginning in 1820, several American colonies were established in Mexico, first with permission from Spain, later with land grants from the Mexican government after Mexico broke with Spain in 1821. By 1836 almost 30,000 American colonists had settled in Texas. Mexican officials became increasingly uncomfortable with the growing number of immigrants, and the government moved to limit them.

In 1834 Mexico's constitutional government was overthrown by the forces of General Antonio Lopez de Santa Anna, who declared himself dictator. The following year the colonists rebelled against Mexico, seeking independence. In December 1835 a team of Texans seized the Alamo from Mexican troops and took control of San Antonio. In response, Santa Anna raised an army of several thousand to retake the territory.

Santa Anna's army reached the area on February 23, 1936 and for thirteen days of siege his artillery bombarded the walls of the mission. On the morning of March 6 his soldiers made their grand assault; they were repulsed in two attacks but on the third they finally overran the defenders.

In April, under Sam Houston, the Texans got their revenge, routing the Mexican army at the Battle of San Jacinto and capturing Santa Anna. Nine years later the independent Republic of Texas became the twenty-eighth state to join the Union.

PLYMOUTH ROCK

{
The Pilgrims crossed the Atlantic on a ship called the *Mayflower* and landed in America at Plymouth Rock in Massachusetts.
Don't you believe it.
}

The Pilgrims did cross the ocean on the *Mayflower* and did land in Massachusetts, but did not at Plymouth Rock. They had originally set sail for the Virginia colony but on their crossing foul weather and heavy winds carried them further north. Persistent bad weather later prevented them from sailing south to their planned destination and they dropped anchor in what is now Providence Harbor on Cape Cod.

A small party was dispatched on foot to explore the surroundings, possibly to find a settlement site. They encountered no inhabitants but found a place where native people had stored corn, which they appropriated to use as seed. But the Pilgrims found both the soil and the water supply poor, so they decided to look elsewhere. One of the *Mayflower*'s officers suggested Plymouth Harbor, which he remembered from a previous voyage, and a search party set out in the *Mayflower*'s small boat. They encountered a storm crossing Cape Cod Bay but finally reached Plymouth, going ashore on December 21, 1620.

They found, according to the writings of William Bradford, later governor of Plymouth Colony, "diverse cornfeilds, & litle runing brooks, a place (as they supposed) fitt for situation; at least it was ye best they could find, and ye season, & their presente necessitie, made them glad to accepte of it. So they returned to their shipp againe with this news to ye rest of their people, which did much comforte their harts."

Most history books don't report that cold and disease soon took over. Of the 102 *Mayflower* passengers only half remained alive by spring.

ROBBING THE MINT

{ US mints are secure. They are so well protected that criminals would not even consider robbing one. **Don't you believe it.** }

Several attempts to rob US mints are on record, most perpetrated by employees. As such they might better be classified as larceny or embezzlement.

In 1893 Philadelphia mint authorities discovered thirty gold bars valued at $130,000 were missing. An employee was sentenced to seven-and-a-half years at hard labor as a result; only $110,000 worth were recovered. In a 1901 audit at the San Francisco mint, six bags of $20 gold eagles could not be located. The chief clerk was convicted and locked up for nine years. The coins never turned up. Late in 1919, $80,000 of gold pieces disappeared from the Denver mint. A worker was caught stealing them in a hollowed out prosthetic wooden leg. He got ten years in federal prison. In September 2011 a Philadelphia mint officer pleaded guilty of stealing $2.4 million of coins. The judge gave him three years in federal penitentiary.

There were also a few forcible robberies. In August 1858 two thieves pilfered $265 in gold pieces from a display case at the Philadelphia mint. They were captured trying to spend the rare coins at local shops.

The most violent mint robbery occurred in 1922 at the Denver mint where a Federal Reserve Bank truck was loading bags of $5 bills, totaling $200,000, when three men in a touring car brandished shotguns and grabbed the money bags. One guard and one of the robbers were killed.

Twelve years later, in 1934, the robbers were identified by the Denver police. Of the five men and two woman who were involved in the robbery only two were still alive, and already in jail.

So in truth the mints are vulnerable, from inside and out.

MAN VERSUS BEAST

{
Gladiators fought only other gladiators in the arena. Animals as antagonists were reserved for slaves, condemned criminals, and war captives.
Don't you believe it.
}

Most fighters thrown into the ring with wild animals were there as a spectacle for the good citizens of Rome in a form of retribution called *damnatio ad bestias* ("damnation to beasts"). For them it was a punishment, not a contest. But there was a special class of gladiators that did fight wild animals; they were a group of warriors called *bestiarii*, pretty much the bottom rung of the gladiatorial fellowship. A *bestiarius* was trained in a special school, the Ludus matutinus in Rome, which taught not only the killing of animals, but also their behavior and habits, and he entered the ring wearing only a loincloth and armed with only a spear.

The finest *bestiarius* of all was named Carpophorus, who in one day killed a bear, a lion, and a panther, then another seventeen wild animals, all in one giant spectacle. He was known to snap the necks of lions and fight them barehanded. Carpophorus also apparently was the only person in recorded Roman history to have killed a leopard, a rare occurrence. No one knows how many animals Carpophorus slayed. It was said that he called the animals by name and could stare them down, holding his ground while none would attack him.

He was so good at dispatching animals that poems were written about him. He was so well known, the crowds were said to scream his name. Martial, in *Spectacles*, has written that if Carpophorus had been alive at time, "Marathon would not have feared the bull, nor leafy Nemea her lion, nor Arcadians the board of Marnalus."

Carpophorus is one of the very few *bestiarii* whose name is remembered.

YET MORE QUICK ONES

The sun seems closer to the Earth in summer, but it's not. In winter the sun is about three million miles nearer to the Earth than in the middle of summer. But the Earth is tilted toward the sun in summer and away from it in winter. So the sun affects us more directly in July and August.

Cleopatra may not have died from the bite of an asp. Some historians believe she committed suicide by drinking poison she carried with her in a container hidden in her hair.

Ten-gallon hats won't hold ten gallons of anything. At full capacity, they can contain less than one gallon.

Whales do not spout water through their blowholes. When whales surface to breathe air, they spout what appears to be a stream of sea water. But it really is air that has been heated in their bodies while they were under water. When exhaled, the warm air from inside meets the cool air over the sea and it condenses to a steamy jet.

The Dead Sea is not a sea; it's a lake.

John Kennedy, at age forty-three, was not the youngest president of the United States. The youngest was Theodore Roosevelt, at forty-two. Kennedy, however, was the youngest to be elected president. Teddy Roosevelt became president after McKinley died from an assassin's bullet on the first of September in 1901.

Movies often show slaves rowing galleys in ancient Rome, but that wasn't done. Only free men were permitted to row; slaves were believed to be too unpredictable. Only when manpower was unavailable were slaves were put at the oars. Condemned criminals were never used as oarsmen, despite the illusion created by films like *Ben-Hur*.

The Romans did not use chariots as battle vehicles. Since both hands were needed to operate the reins, the rider did not have a free hand to wield a weapon.

The famous Woodstock Festival wasn't held in Woodstock, New York. It was held in New York State, but in the town of Bethel, over forty miles southwest of Woodstock.

HOLIDAY SONGS

{ Many Christian holidays have inspired popular songs that memorialize the day. So it would not be unreasonable to assume that many of the anthems would likely have been created by devotees of the Church. **Don't you believe it.** }

The most widely known popular songs glorifying Christian religious holidays were written, rather, by a non-Christian Russian immigrant to the United States, a man named Israel Isidor Baline. Israel Baline came to the United States at age five; he died at age 101 on September 1989 in New York City. In the intervening ninety-six years he wrote over 2,000 songs, several universally recognized, won many awards, and changed his name to Irving Berlin. Irving Berlin happened to be Jewish.

Berlin's best known festival songs are "Easter Parade," "Happy Holiday," and "White Christmas," all widely played during the appropriate holiday season. But he can also claim credit for several patriotic tunes for his adopted country, many helping the war effort in two world wars; such as "Any Bonds Today," "I Left My Heart at the Stage Door Canteen," "Oh! How I Hate to Get Up in the Morning," "For Your Country," and "My Country," and the quintessential statement of patriotic fervor, "God Bless America," for which he was awarded the Congressional Gold Medal.

Oddly, though Berlin was the author and composer of several hundreds of songs, he never learned to read music. "Why bother learning to read it," he once said, "I'm too busy writing it."

Interesting that Christian holidays and American patriotism are best illuminated by the works of a non-Christian, non-native American. Berlin's story is truly a tribute to American pluralism and how people from disparate cultures can learn to live together and absorb one another's ethos.

THE KILT

{ The kilt is a short, pleated plaid skirt invented by and worn by Scotsmen, only in Scotland and only by men. **Don't you believe it.** }

The kilt was invented about 1727 by an Englishman from Lancashire named Thomas Rawlinson. It is an abbreviated version of a larger full-body garment called the belted plaid (sometimes *the great kilt*), the bottom half separated from the top and worn independently. It is also known as the small kilt or *philibeg*.

Rawlinson was running a business near Inverness in the early eighteenth century, producing charcoal and smelting iron ore. He suspected his workers' performances were impeded by their unwieldy apparel, and he thought to increase their efficiency by reducing the baggage they wore. The resulting lesser kilt soon caught on with Highland workers when they saw it worn by Rawlinson and his Scottish partner.

First associated with the poor Highland clans, the kilt was scorned by the more affluent clans. Later, when Scottish regiments in kilts fought for the British Empire, the attitude toward the Scots began to change. By the late nineteenth century it was the affluent who were photographed in kilts, even in the Lowland cities of Glasgow and Edinburgh, and the kilt became national attire.

There is some evidence of Highlanders wearing only the lower half of the belted plaid in the late 1700s, but without the sewn-in pleats, which are characteristic of Rawlinson's small kilt.

Kilts also appeared in Ireland, but a distinguishable form from the Scottish variety. A Scottish kilt is traditionally made from the family tartan, the Irish kilt is either in a solid color or a tartan representing the Irish county of the family's origin. Although not part of national costume, kilts have become popular in other Celtic nations as a sign of Celtic identity.

WALKING UNDER A LADDER

{ Walking under a ladder is considered unlucky because the likelihood is high that something will drop on the walker.
Don't you believe it. }

Yes, a person crossing under an open ladder risks being bombarded with paint or a tool or a board or a lighting fixture or whatever else is being worked at the top of the ladder. But that doesn't seem to qualify the bombardee as unlucky. Adventurous, maybe, or imprudent, or daring—all seem more to the point than "unlucky." Good luck is encouraged by good judgment. To paraphrase an old saying, "You can't burn yourself if you don't play with fire."

But in any case, that is not the source of the well-known superstition. Rather, the belief has a few interlocking antecedents, some dating back to pre-Christian times. A ladder leaning against a wall forms a triangle, a classic symbol of life. Walking through its space was considered hazardous to your future and was sure to have bad repercussions. The shape of a ladder leaning against a wall also resembled a gallows, a device of obvious bad luck. This was another long-standing imputed association. According to ancient prescriptions, to neutralize the evil spirit of the gallows it was necessary to spit three times, through the rungs of the ladder.

But perhaps the governing symbol of the open triangle was that of the Holy Trinity, the Father, the Son, and the Holy Spirit. The superstitious thought that walking under a ladder—through boundaries of the Holy Trinity—displayed disbelief in the Trinity and therefore implied an alliance with the devil. Executing such an act would be suspicious and possibly invite being named a witch, which would have been extremely perilous.

So the physical dangers of an accident were far less foreboding than the less tangible spiritual dangers.

UNITED NATIONS LOCATION

{
The property in New York City on which the United Nations is built was donated to the UN by John D. Rockefeller as an expression of his philanthropic largess.

Don't you believe it.
}

There may have been an altruistic component to Rockefeller's benevolence, but his proposal to donate the land was more a business decision.

The seventeen acres on which the UN complex was constructed had previously been an area of slaughterhouses and a railroad garage, all accumulated by land developer named William Zeckendorf, one of Rockefeller's most zealous competitors. Zeckendorf had purchased the land with the intention of constructing a city-within-a-city to rival Rockefeller Center, a district for business, tourism, and cultural activity, a "dream city" with its own transportation system and distinctive design. His plan called for a multimillion-dollar complex of several office buildings, hotels, and apartment houses, supported by theaters, shopping areas, a marina, and, of course, a rooftop airport. He anticipated a major impact on New York City with the relocation and absorption of the Metropolitan Opera and a floating restaurant/nightclub. Such a zone would surely diminish the distinctive allurement of Rockefeller Center as a place to visit and do business in.

But like many of Zeckendorf's expansive schemes, his financing didn't keep pace with his implementation and he soon developed money problems. Which gave Rockefeller the opportunity to advance his reputation for civic responsibility while at the same time eliminating likely business competition. Nelson, John D.'s son, managed to buy the seventeen acres for $8.5 million and the senior Rockefeller donated it to the UN, for which he took on a whole new reserve of renown as the American who gave the United Nations its home.

DID ROOSEVELT KNOW?

{
The Japanese bombing of Pearl Harbor caught the US totally off guard. No one in the American government or military had any foreknowledge of what Japan was planning.
Maybe . . . Maybe not.
}

The commanders at Pearl Harbor certainly did not, but some revisionist historians believe that President Roosevelt likely did. They cite, for example, an official phone call from Winston Churchill in late November informing the president that Japan had moved several aircraft carriers eastward across the Pacific and would likely attack Pearl Harbor within the following two weeks. Roosevelt did nothing. A declassified memorandum from the Office of Naval Intelligence dated December 4 warned the President that Japan was viewing Hawaii with an eye toward "open conflict." Roosevelt did nothing.

Japanese navy dispatches and diplomatic exchanges were decoded but not shared with our commanders at Pearl Harbor. On December 1–2, worldwide Japanese embassies in non-Axis nations were directed to dispose of their secret documents and all but one copy of their codes, something that is done just prior to hostile action.

It is believed that Roosevelt did not act on his knowledge because he wanted the US to enter the war and by doing so become a player on the international stage. And he could not reveal to the Japanese that their codes had been broken. But it was necessary that the Japanese be the aggressors so that their actions would enrage America, and especially the isolationists, to support US entry into the war. On November 25 Secretary of War Henry Stimson wrote in his diary: "The question was how we should maneuver them [the Japanese] into the position of firing the first shot . . ."

After several national inquiries we still do not know what FDR knew.

MAO'S GREAT LEAP FORWARD

{ Chairman Mao Zedong's "Great Leap Forward" really was a great leap forward for China. **Don't you believe it.** }

In 1958, with relations between China and the USSR souring, Chairman Mao realized that China had to stand alone to modernize its predominantly agrarian society to a contemporary industrial one. His plan was to restructure agriculture and industry to grow together, each supporting the other. Industry could advance only if the workers were well fed so they could produce the tools needed to increase production of food, and other necessary products.

Mao's wish was to update China's economy to match that of the United States in a Great Leap Forward. To accomplish this, 700 million citizens were organized into thousands of agricultural collectives. Targets were set and the people were urged to beat them. Other projects were completed ahead of schedule, but frequently of inferior quality. Mao also urged the peasants to build backyard blast furnaces to melt down scrap metal to make iron for useful items, like tools and utensils. But the program turned contrary; when they ran out of scrap metal people began melting down useful items, including tools and utensils, to produce unusable stores of metal.

Through mismanagement, misguided economic policy, and adverse weather conditions, the plan was a disaster. An estimated thirty to forty million Chinese died, most from starvation in the countryside.

It was supposed to be a five-year plan, but it was terminated after three calamitous years. In China, the period from 1958–60 is now referred to as "Three Bitter Years."

INDULGING TERRORISTS

{
The United States will never negotiate with terrorists, never ransom political prisoners, nor make concessions to insurgents.
Don't you believe it.
}

The US government has a firm policy never to deal with terrorists—never ever. Until, that is, a deal is made.

One particularly notorious exception occurred in 1986, when President Reagan facilitated the sale of arms to Iran—though an embargo on such sale was in force—and used that income to finance the Contras opposing the communist Sandinista government of Nicaragua—which was also illegal, and specifically forbidden by Congress. But President Reagan considered the Contras to be "the moral equivalent of our founding fathers," even though they had a long history of disregard for human rights.

The episode became known as the "Iran-Contra affair," the arms transfer to Iran intended as a quid pro quo for the release of hostages held in Lebanon by a group tied to the Iranis. The Contras were not an intact force, but a cluster of several right-of-center Nicaraguan groups allied only in their opposition to the left-wing government. A report commissioned by the State Department found Reagan's assertion of Soviet influence in Nicaragua to be "exaggerated." The two activities were independent covert operations, related only by propinquity.

The International Court of Justice found that the US had violated international law by supporting the Contras, by mining Nicaragua's harbors, and by encouraging violation of humanitarian law in its publication and distribution of the manual *Psychological Operations in Guerilla Warfare*. The manual, among other things, rationalized killing civilians.

It was a complex arrangement, both supporting and opposing insurgencies. Both, however, contrary to explicit US policy.

PIRATE JEAN LAFITTE DEFENDS NEW ORLEANS

> Pirate Jean Lafitte and his buccaneers fought along-side the American forces in the Battle of New Orleans, defeating the British in the decisive final action in the War of 1812.
> **Don't you believe it.**

The War of 1812 pitted the United States against Great Britain and its allied Native American tribes. American belligerence toward Great Britain was provoked by the Royal Navy's impressment of American merchant seamen into the British fleet, by British trade restrictions growing out of its war with France, and by US desire to expropriate British land in Canada. The United States declared war on June 18, 1812.

America endured several defeats over two-and-a-half years of the war, notably the August 1814 burning of Washington, DC. Nonetheless, American forces were able to repel British incursions into New York and Baltimore. The British then turned their attention to invading the South via New Orleans. When Major-General Andrew Jackson took command of the American forces in New Orleans, he found poorly trained, ill-equipped troops and not enough seamen to man the ships that had been seized from Lafitte's brigands on their capture. In exchange for US pardons, Lafitte and his pirates joined Jackson in the defense of New Orleans.

Lafitte's men helped turn the battle against the King's forces in the most devastating clash of the war, starting on January 8, when Jackson's ragtag army faced twice as many King's regulars and repulsed them with disastrous losses.

But the victory had no effect on the outcome of the war; one month earlier, on December 24, 1814, the United States and Great Britain had signed the Treaty of Ghent, ending the war before the battle began.

ROGER WILLIAMS

> Roger Williams is remembered as a Puritan minister who was one of the leaders of the Massachusetts Bay Colony.
> **Don't you believe it.**

Yes, Williams was a minister in the Bay Colony, until he fell from favor for his rejection of Puritan intolerance of other religions and his objection to appropriating land from the Native Americans. For his dissent he was tried and convicted of sedition and heresy, the colony Court declaring that he was promoting "diverse, new, and dangerous opinions." He was sentenced to banishment from the Colony, but before the authorities could administer the sentence he managed to slip away.

Williams found his way to Narragansett Bay, where he and his followers purchased land from the Narragansett Indians in 1636 and founded a new settlement named Providence Plantations, dedicated to religious liberty and the notion of a "wall of separation" between the church and the state. Combining with other nearby settlements to create the colony of Rhode Island in 1644, the new enlarged polity became a haven for religious minorities, instituting a government rooted in the protection of individual "liberty of conscience." While other colonies also respected religious toleration, Rhode Island was the only one created with this as the objective.

Propounding withdrawal of fidelity to the Church of England, an institution which he deemed irredeemably corrupt and false, he taught that individual worship was the only true route to a relation with God. He held that liberty and the right of ethical choice are both divinely inspired and that freedom of religion is a natural right requiring that the church and the state remain separate.

His ideas about the relation between religion and government were adopted into the First Amendment to the Constitution.

A TRANSVESTITE
NEW YORK GOVERNOR

{ The colony of New York once had a cross-dresser as its governor.
You can believe it. }

Edward Hyde, Viscount Cornbury, was appointed by the Crown as governor of the colonies of New York and New Jersey in 1701. Cornbury was a nephew of James II and a cousin of the future Queen Anne. But as an Anglican, he deserted James and pledged allegiance to William III, for which he was given the prestigious commission in the New World.

Cornbury quickly achieved a reputation as the "worst governor Britain ever imposed on an American colony." He was morally and socially corrupt, venal, arrogant, and inept. And he wore dresses, especially at official functions.

He is reputed to have convened the 1702 New York Assembly wearing an ornate gown and carrying an ornamented fan. When questioned about his choice of apparel, he is said to have replied, "You are all very stupid people not to see the propriety of it all in this place and occasion. I represent a woman, the Queen, and in all respects I ought to represent her as faithfully as I can."

A portrait of a man in elegant woman's clothes is on display the New York Historical Society. It is identified as *Viscount Cornbury, governor of New York and New Jersey* (1702–1708).

In 1708, after several years of looting the public treasury and ignoring his settler's needs, Cornbury was dumped as governor, arrested for unpaid debts, and imprisoned for seventeen months. When his father died, his inheritance enabled him to pay his debts and return to England to regain his reputation. He never did.

New York University historian Patricia Bonomi in her 1998 book, *The Lord Cornbury Scandal*, holds that much of this story is myth, a libel spread by political enemies of Cornbury, as is that infamous painting of him.

True or untrue, it's a good story.

ADMIRAL FARRAGUT LASHED TO THE MAST

{ During the Civil War's Battle of Mobile Bay in August 1864, Union Rear Admiral David Farragut famously lashed himself to the mast to display his intent to go down with his ship if his ship indeed had to go down.
Don't you believe it. }

Yes, Admiral Farragut was lashed to the rigging, but the act wasn't one of defiance. Rather it was a strategic move in the midst of a loud and hazy battle. With the smoke from the guns obscuring the action, Farragut climbed into the rigging to get a better view of what was happening. He climbed high enough to be severely wounded if he should fall to the deck. The captain of the ship ordered a sailor aloft with a line to secure him, but he told the sailor it wasn't necessary. Nonetheless the seaman followed his captain's order and tied Farragut to the ship's shrouds.

Farragut was stationed on his flagship *Hartford* in command of an eighteen-ship flotilla with the mission to close Mobile Bay to blockade runners. Entering the bay his fleet was severely bombarded by forts Gaines and Morgan, which were positioned to protect the entrance to the harbor. After passing out of range of the shore batteries, Farragut forced the Confederate naval forces to surrender, effectively shutting down Mobile Bay. Mobile had been the last important port in Confederate hands on the Gulf of Mexico east of the Mississippi River, so its shutdown completed the closure of Confederate ports in that region, cutting off one of the South's sources of supply.

This is the same action that produced a memorable battle cry known to every American school child. To enter the bay, Farragut had to take his fleet through a field of mines known then as torpedoes—and in a rash but heroic order told his crew, "Damn the torpedoes! Full speed ahead!"

SWANEE RIVER

Stephen Foster first sang of the Swanee River in his song "Old Folks at Home." George Gershwin and Irving Caesar later eulogized it in their tune called entitled simply "Swanee," which Al Jolson sang and popularized, helping, as the saying goes, to put it on the map.
Don't you believe it.

It's a nice remembrance, but it's of a place that never existed. Search as many maps as you can find and you'll never locate a river named Swanee. Al Jolson advises, or, depending on your point of view, threatens, "the folks up North will see me no more when I get to that Swanee shore." Small wonder: there is no Swanee shore, no Swanee for the old folks' home, and definitely no Swanee River.

There is a Sewanee University in Tennessee that calls itself "The University of the South." There were the Siwanoy Indians, who lived in the Bronx area now called Mott Haven, known for their massacre of Anne Hutchinson and her family. There's Sweeney, a venerable Irish name. There's Dabo Swinney, head coach of the Clemson football team. There's a Swansea City in Wales, known for its soccer club. There's swami, a title for a Hindu religious teacher. There's a Suwanee River in Northern Florida and southern Georgia. But no Swanee anything.

So where did the name in the song originate? Sources reveal that Stephen Foster was writing about the Suwanee River but had to abbreviate the name to get it to fit the meter of his song. Artistic license. But why did Gershwin and Caesar choose to alter the name in the same way? We can only speculate. Nevertheless, over time, the Swanee, which never existed, is better known than the Suwanee, which is actually there.

And the word is that Stephen Foster never even saw the river he celebrated.

THE TRANSCONTINENTAL RAILROAD

{
The transcontinental railroad, completed in 1869, linked the west coast of the United States to the east coast.
Don't you believe it.
}

The completed railroad, though called "transcontinental," wasn't. Its eastern terminus was far from the Atlantic coast. At the time, there was no crossing the Mississippi River without a boat, so the east end of the line began west of the Mississippi, in Council Bluffs, Iowa. From there, one needed other connections to reach the east coast.

The plan called for construction by two different companies, the Central Pacific Railroad, building from west to east, and the Union Pacific Railroad east to west, to meet at some as-yet-undetermined location. The builders were paid by the mile, so a fierce competition developed between them, each frantically adding as many miles as possible. But without a predetermined junction of the separate lines, the two builders were soon grading land for track on parallel routes. Congress stepped in and demanded they decide on a meeting place; they chose Promontory Summit in Utah territory.

After six years of construction, the last link was added between inland Sacramento and Oakland on San Francisco Bay. And the final coupling of east and west was celebrated with the famous Golden Spike on May 10, 1869, resulting in a 1,907-mile continuous railroad line that provided a vital link for trade and travel, and brought the western states and territories into the Union.

Eventually known as the Overland Route, the new pathway offered integration of the agricultural abundance of the west with the markets of the east, stimulated a plethora of new towns along the railroad corridor, and gave the people an optimistic belief that anything was possible in the new nation.

But the trans was short of continental.

THE US ARMY VERSUS US CIVILIANS

{ The Kent State fiasco was the first and only time that American troops used force against American civilians.
Don't you believe it. }

The Kent State incident, in which university students during the Korean War demonstrated against the government's bombing Cambodia, took the lives of four students, two demonstrators, and two innocents crossing the campus. Nine other students were wounded.

But there were prior instances. There was Shays' rebellion in 1786–7, instigated by debtor farmers in Massachusetts unable to sell their harvest or pay their taxes because of the debt crisis growing out of the Revolutionary War. Farmers had functioned in a barter economy and couldn't raise the cash to pay their debts. When foreclosures became common, the farmers revolted. Four were killed and a few score wounded.

And over the years, the military or National Guard was used frequently to break labor strikes, many such actions resulting in one or two deaths. The Posse Comitatus Law of 1878 was intended to keep the military out of law enforcement activities.

But the largest confrontation between military forces and civilians occurred in 1932 when some 40,000—about 20,000 veterans of WWI and their families—gathered in the capitol, demanding payment of bonuses promised them for their service in the war. The World War Adjusted Compensation Act of 1924 had voted a bonus should be awarded to World War I veterans, $1.25 for each day served overseas and $1.00 for each day in the States. But there was a caveat attached—payment would not be made until 1945; in the interim each account would accumulate interest. Many of these veterans were also victims of the Depression and felt that the Smoot-Hawley Tariff Act had already given industry a competitive "bonus" by imposing tariffs on imported goods. They wanted theirs now when they needed it.

The Bonus Army made camp wherever they could find space. The largest encampment, soon named Hooverville, was built on the Anacostia Flats, across the river from the central federal area. Shelters were built from whatever trash could be found nearby—scrap lumber, shipping crates, and abandoned packing boxes, all covered with roofs of discarded tin panels. The camp came to resemble a small village with named streets, a barber shop, a library, even a post office. They also issued their own newspaper.

The veterans were heartened when the House of Representatives passed the Patman Bonus Bill Act on June 15, despite President Hoover's vow to veto it. But on June 17 the Senate voted it down, and several thousand veterans refused to leave Washington. After a few skirmishes between the squatters and police, President Hoover ordered the Secretary of War to "surround the affected area and clear it without delay." On July 28, US Attorney General William D. Mitchell ordered the veterans "removed from all government property."

Army Chief of Staff General MacArthur was convinced that the enterprise was a communist conspiracy to undermine the government of the United States. He overstepped his orders, took personal command and cleared the camp with tanks, cavalry, and soldiers utilizing tear gas. The Bonus Army marchers with their wives and children were driven out, their shelters and belongings burned.

Fortunately, the death toll was limited to two veterans.

PURITAN CHRISTMAS

{ The Puritans who settled in America, a notably devout
group, would have celebrated Christmas as an integral
part of their religious observance.
Don't you believe it. }

Christmas was a no-no for the Puritans. In fact, they instituted
a law in 1659 prohibiting its observance and levying a fine of
five shillings from anyone "found observing, by abstinence from
labor, feasting, or any other way, any such days as Christmas day."
This was in line with dictates of the Cromwell regime in England
which had outlawed the holiday as "residual Papist idolatry."

The Puritans considered the celebration of Christmas "an
extreme forgetfulness of Christ, by giving liberty to carnal and
sensual delights" and found no justification in scripture for its
observance. Besides, they were unconvinced of the date of Jesus's
birth, believing December 25 was ahistorical, merely the perpetu-
ation of a Roman festival date. Puritans called the celebration of
Christmas "Foolstide" and saw it as representing paganism and
idolatry. The only holy day they found sanctioned in scripture was
the Sabbath.

Christmas celebrations were illegal throughout Britain
during most of the seventeenth century. Christmas festivities in
Britain had become raucous and disorderly, with drunkenness and
promiscuity as typical activities; the holiday had come to encom-
pass the concept of *misrule*, i.e., a formalized reversal of accepted
social norms. The Puritans strove to focus on group piety and
banish all residuals of Roman Catholicism.

When Christmas was declared a federal holiday in 1870,
the Puritan view quickly faded and since late in the nineteenth
century, Christmas has taken on its present contradictory character of spirituality and commercialism.

BOULDER DAM

{ The giant dam on the Colorado River at the Arizona-Nevada border, about forty-five miles from Las Vegas, sometimes known as Hoover Dam, was originally named Boulder Dam because it is built in Boulder Canyon.
Don't you believe it. }

Actually, the dam sits astride Black Canyon, not Boulder Canyon. When originally planned, the dam was to be built in Boulder Canyon and thus named the Boulder Canyon Project. But early soundings discovered too many serious faults in the land where the dam was to be constructed, so the construction site was moved to nearby Black Canyon. Still, based on its original plans, the dam was familiarly referred to as Boulder Dam, even though when the project had been inaugurated in 1930 Secretary of the Interior Ray L. Wilbur proclaimed the structure would be called Hoover Dam, honoring the sitting president.

With Hoover's defeat in 1932 and the Roosevelt administration taking over the government in 1933, the Hoover name, in an apparently political decision, was dropped and the structure once again became the Boulder Dam. Later, when Roosevelt's Secretary of the Interior Harold Ickes spoke at the dedication ceremony at its completion on September 30, 1935, he made a concerted effort, as he wrote in his diary, "to try to nail down for good and all the name Boulder Dam." In his remarks, Roosevelt also spoke of Boulder Dam.

In the years following, neither name caught on widely. Both were used interchangeably; even geographers could not settle on a definitive name. Until, that is, 1947, at which time the title was finalized when both houses of Congress voted to re-establish the name Hoover Dam. But the Boulder name has not been lost; some people, no doubt drawing on old information or unbending predilection, still refer to it as such.

FERDINAND MAGELLAN

{ Ferdinand Magellan was the first explorer to sail around the world, or, in the patois of school history, to circumnavigate the globe.
Don't you believe it. }

In September 1519 Magellan, a skilled Portuguese captain sailing under the Spanish flag, left Seville searching for a westward route to the Spice Islands (the Moluccas). Spices in the sixteenth century were a key component of the international economy, prized both for flavoring and preserving food. And since Europe's climate prohibited cultivation at home, practicality dictated finding the quickest sea route to their source in Indonesia. The eastbound corridor was known, but no one had yet searched for a shorter course by sailing west, which might prove more economical. Magellan was determined to discover if that route existed.

Magellan's fleet of five ships and a crew of 270 departed Spain, setting sail for South America, which they reached in early December. While there, Magellan put down a mutiny and lost one ship in a scouting expedition; the remaining fleet crossed the continent in a narrow channel that what came to be called the Strait of Magellan, and then entered a large body of water he named the "peaceful sea" (the Pacific Ocean). Heading northwest, the expedition, down to 150 men, reached the island of Cebu in the Philippines in mid-March 1521. There Magellan fell into an inter-island conflict and was killed in a battle on Mactan.

After his death the two surviving ships sailed to the Moluccas and loaded up on spices. One then headed unsuccessfully back across the Pacific Ocean while the other, the *Vittoria*, continued west, through the Indian Ocean, around the Cape of Good Hope, and arrived in Spain in September 1522, only eighteen of the original 270 voyagers returning. So while his expedition had sailed around the world, Magellan himself did not.

FDR AND THE GREAT DEPRESSION

{
President Roosevelt's New Deal programs ended the Great Depression that had begun in 1929.
Don't you believe it.
}

The Great Depression that followed the stock market crash on October 24, 1929—Black Thursday—was the longest and most pervasive economic downturn in our nation's history. President Hoover told the American people that the crisis would pass, but it only got worse. By 1930 some four million people were looking for jobs where none existed. By 1931 the number had reached six million. Soup kitchens and bread lines were in fashion around the country. By 1933, 25 percent of the US labor force was unemployed and half the country's banks had failed.

In 1932 Democrat Franklin D. Roosevelt won an overwhelming victory for the presidency, and on assuming office he instituted a package of programs meant to alleviate the widespread suffering and put people back to work. When he uttered his famous declaration, "We have nothing to fear but fear itself," his positive attitude gave the country hope for better times. His new agencies did manage to moderate the downward spiral in American business and to stimulate hiring, putting four million people back to work. But more than twice that number still could not find jobs.

In the years that followed, the American economy gradually improved and unemployment began to abate, until the sharp downturn during the recession of 1937–38, when manufacturing output dropped more than 35 percent, back to 1934 levels, and unemployment spiked 5 percent upward. Slightly offsetting the loss in employment was the continuing modest increase in wages.

But the depression didn't end until the country adopted a wartime economy in the late 1930s. It was World War II, not Roosevelt's intercession, which ended the Great Depression.

JOHN GLENN IN SPACE

{ John Glenn was the first American astronaut in space. **Don't you believe it.** }

Colonel Glenn was not the first American in space. That distinction belongs to Alan Shephard, another of the original NASA Mercury Seven astronauts. Nor was Glenn the second; that was Gus Grissom. John Glenn's achievement was piloting the *Friendship 7* Mercury spacecraft in the first US-manned orbital flight.

Glenn performed his successful three-orbit mission around the Earth on February 20, 1962. The flight recorded a maximum altitude of 162 statute miles and an orbital velocity of about 17,000 miles per hour. Launched from Kennedy Space Center on the east coast of Florida, his flight time was four hours, fifty-five minutes, and twenty-three seconds until his splashdown near Grand Turk Island in the Caribbean Sea.

John Herschel Glenn Jr. had been a Marine Corps pilot who saw service in the South Pacific late in World War II, and was promoted to captain before the war's end. He distinguished himself in the Korean War flying sixty-three combat missions and displaying a penchant for attracting enemy flak. On two missions his plane returned to base showing over 250 holes. In a second Korean tour, he completed twenty-seven missions and shot down three MiGs. Among the honors he received for his service in 149 combat missions in two wars he was awarded the Distinguished Flying Cross and the Air Medal with eighteen clusters.

Glenn retired from NASA in January 1964, and in 1974 was elected to the US Senate, serving until 1999. But his flying days were not over. In October 1998, still a sitting senator, he became the oldest person in space when, at age seventy-seven, he flew as a Payload Specialist on Discovery's STS-95 mission.

With the death of Scott Carpenter in October 2013, Glenn became the last surviving member of the Mercury Seven. He died in Columbus, Ohio, on December 8, 2016.

DISNEY BANNED

{
Disney film cartoons, usually described as wholesome, have never sparked even a suggestion of offending public propriety.
Don't you believe it.
}

A Mickey Mouse cartoon called *The Shindig* was banned in the state of Ohio in 1931. The film opens with Clarabelle Cow lying on her bed reading a book entitled *Three Weeks,* a titillating novel that had been declared obscene, was banned in Boston and Canada, and condemned by religious leaders in the United States. It was the work of Elinor Glyn, a British novelist and screenwriter who was known as a mainstay of women's mass-market erotic fiction. Glyn was notorious for having had affairs with several British aristocrats. *Three Weeks,* allegedly inspired by her liaison with a much younger peer, had scandalized Edwardian society. Incidentally, it was Elinor Glyn who adapted the word "it" to stand for "sex appeal," a racy notion for America in the 1920s.

But that was not why the film distressed Ohioans. In the film, while Clarabelle is reading, a knock on the door announces the arrival of her date, Horace Horsecollar, at which time Clarabelle gets off her bed and dresses. Which implied that we had just been watching a naked cow reading a risqué book. In covering the incident, *Time* magazine reported that the state of Ohio banned *The Shindig* because it showed a cow's teats. I suspect it was not simply the display of her udder, but rather its immensity that prompted Ohioan's discomfort.

But the event did have repercussions. According to a 1931 article in *Time,* "Cows in Mickey Mouse . . . pictures in the future will have small or invisible udders quite unlike the gargantuan organ whose antics of late have shocked some and convulsed others."

Still, it is a mystery how this stuff made it into a Disney film.

AGAIN, QUICK ONES

The lion isn't king of the jungle. He doesn't even live in the jungle. The lion's natural habitat is grassland or open woodland. Nor is he the family's provider; the lioness does most of the hunting for the pride. The male in the pride usually remains behind and tends the cubs until the lioness returns from the hunt.

Indictment is not the finding of guilt of the accused person. Rather, it is the initiation of official charges against a public official.

The Eiffel Tower, installed for the 1889 Universal Exposition in Paris, was issued a time-limited license by the city to occupy its site for twenty years, after which it was to be removed. But in 1909 the army and the French telegraph officials persuaded the city to cancel the demolition because the radio antenna on top of the tower was vital for the transmission of essential messages. The tower remains.

In 1938 *Time* magazine named Hitler as Man of the Year.

Oddly enough, heavy cream weighs less than light cream. It contains more fat, which weighs less than the equivalent amount of water.

Head cheese isn't a type of cheese. It is meat from the head of a pig or calf, boiled, then chopped, and mixed with gelatin in a mold, served cold.

Reaching the moon wasn't a noble ideal for President Kennedy. It was purely a political decision to beat the Russians for our national pride and international prestige.

President Grover Cleveland, our twenty-second and twenty-fourth presidents, had been known as the "Buffalo Hangman" while sheriff of Erie County, New York State, in the 1870s. He is known to have executed at least two prisoners.

MARTIN LUTHER

{ Martin Luther, as the story goes, initiated the Protestant Reformation by nailing his famous ninety-five theses (objections) to the door of the Wittenberg Catholic Church in October 1517.
Don't you believe it. }

True, Luther did frame a list of grievances, but they were not about the Church in general; rather, they were specifically about the Church's sale of indulgences, which allowed violators to invalidate their sins by feeding the Church's coffers. The amount of "contribution" varied with the deed, conforming to a sliding scale of sin-costs covering pretty much all transgressions.

But Luther never did nail anything to any church door, or any other door. Rather, he sent copies of his complaints to a select few influential figures in hopes of effecting some change. The most consequential recipient was the Archbishop of Mainz, the seat of the Chancellor of the Holy Roman Empire, a questionable designation in that it was neither Holy, nor Roman, and nor really an Empire. Luther had nonetheless made his point and now awaited a response.

The response soon came, from of all people the king, Henry VIII, who excoriated him in a pamphlet, *Declaration of the Seven Sacraments Against Martin Luther*, so caustic that the Pope, Leo X, honored Henry with the title "Fidei Defensor" (Defender of the Faith). (The honorarium was later revoked after Henry split from the Papacy to establish the Church of England.)

In his private life Luther was, in the appraisal of writer Graeme Donald, in his book, *Lies, Damned Lies and History*, "egalitarian" in "the equal spread of his hatreds and prejudices: he was racist, misogynistic, misanthropic, xenophobic and reserved a special dislike for the poor." And notably anti-Semitic, describing Jews as a "base and whoring people."

So much for the virtuous holy man.

MOUNT VESUVIUS

{ In AD 79 the Mount Vesuvius volcano erupted, inundating two cities, Pompeii and Herculaneum, with waves of lava.
Don't you believe it. }

Both cities were destroyed, but neither could blame lava for its demise. The cities suffered different types of ruination: Pompeii, southwest of Vesuvius, was submerged in a sea of ash and pumice stone. Herculaneum, to the northwest, between two streams that flowed down from Vesuvius, was buried in a flood of mud-carrying ash. Despite the almost universal belief than the two cities were done in by lava, archeologists are certain that lava was not the destructive force; if it had been, the lava would have burned up the artifacts that were later found preserved on the sites.

The two cities were very dissimilar. Herculaneum, which had been settled by the Greeks, was an upscale seaside resort city of intellectual pursuits and cultured leisure, noticeably wealthier than Pompeii and in better circumstance, with 5,000 inhabitants. Pompeii owed its origin to Oscan elements of Indo-European ancestry; its 11,000 residents lived in humbler urban dwellings, their only apparent interest being commerce. The most striking commonality of the two was the widespread display of erotic art, found in profusion everywhere in both venues.

Both cities were lost for over 1,500 years. Pompeii was rediscovered first, in 1599, when an underground channel was being dug to divert the local river. But a first view of uncovered art was embarrassing and the site was left undisturbed. In 1748, it was again rediscovered and intentionally excavated. Herculaneum was found in 1709 while a well was being dug and excavation begun in 1738. Pompeii had accumulated a covering of about twelve to fifteen feet of debris, Herculaneum about eighty feet.

At this time, neither has been fully excavated.

THE NRA

{
The National Rifle Association has always advocated uncontrolled ownership of guns.
Don't you believe it.
}

The NRA, instituted in 1871, has not always supported the unrestricted rights of gun owners beyond government regulation. Founded by Colonel William C. Church and General George Wingate, later of the Union forces in the Civil War, who were alarmed by the inadequate shooting skills of army riflemen, the organization was created to provide marksmanship programs. Also intended to educate for responsible gun ownership, the NRA originally condoned gun control measures, even supporting the 1934 National Firearms Act, the first federal gun-control law.

During congressional hearings on the NFA, then NRA President Karl Frederick testified, "I have never believed in the general practice of carrying weapons. I seldom carry one . . . I do not believe in the general promiscuous toting of guns. I think it should be sharply restricted and only under licenses." The NRA also supported the Gun Control Act of 1968, which expanded the government's authority to deny firearm ownership by criminals and those with mental impairment.

But the NRA changed its tone in 1977 when the leadership was assumed by Harlon Carter, a dedicated advocate of limitless gun ownership, at which time the association began its unyielding Second Amendment Rights agenda. The courts generally agreed with this unlimited prerogative to own firearms. Until, that is, June 6, 2016, when a federal eleven-judge panel of the Ninth Circuit Court in San Francisco ruled that the Second Amendment of the Constitution did not include the right to carry a concealed weapon in public without "good cause," a finding likely to be challenged by gun enthusiasts. As of this writing, we will not have the final word on this issue until the decision is review by a higher court.

WOMEN IN COMBAT

{ The American ethos does not countenance women
serving in combat.
Don't you believe it. }

That had been true, but is no longer.

The history of the American Revolution contains several
instances of women fighting alongside men in battle. Think Molly
Pitcher, or Deborah Sampson. But when the Continental mili-
tias were disbanded after the Treaty of Paris, the old expedients
went with them. With the establishment of the US Army in June
1784, the US Navy in March 1794, and the Marines in July 1798,
women were excluded from combat positions.

The arguments for keeping women out of combat are well
known. First, of course, they lack the physical strength needed
to accomplish combat tasks, including removing wounded troops
from the battlefield. Nor could women supposedly handle the
mental strain of the combat situation. Introducing women into
all-men units would degrade cohesion and morale. Then there
was the potential distraction if a woman was wounded: would the
men attend to their military mission or go to her aid? And there
was always the chance that romantic relationships could weaken
a unit's fighting capacity. And so *The Ground Combat Exclusion
Policy*, barring women from combat positions, was formalized in
the Women's Armed Services Integration Act of 1948.

In 1994, the Pentagon updated the *Policy*: "Service members
are eligible to be assigned to all positions for which they are quali-
fied, except that women shall be excluded from assignment to
units below the brigade level whose primary mission is to engage
in direct combat on the ground." Nonetheless, in the Middle East,
without authority, American service women frequently found
themselves in the ill-defined area between the front lines and rear
support, performing combat tasks. These women understandably
were irritated by the combat restrictions which allowed them to

serve in combat zones, often under fire, but disallowed them from filling approved combat positions, including in the infantry, which furthered career advancement.

Additionally, some argued, by excluding women from combat roles, the American government appeared to support a military that treats women as second-class citizens. *The Combat Exclusion Policy* was vacated as of January 24, 2013, adopting a unanimous recommendation by the Joint Chiefs of Staff. Both men and women would now be eligible to serve in front-line combat operations. Then-Defense Secretary Leon Panetta said that the ban was eliminated because "If members of our military can meet the qualifications for a job, then they should have the right to serve, regardless of creed, color, gender or sexual orientation."

In December 2015, Defense Secretary Ashton Carter proclaimed that starting in 2016 all combat jobs would open to women, and he authorized the military to begin integrating female combat soldiers. The Chairman of the Joint Chiefs of Staff, General Joseph Dunford of the Marine Corps dissented, wanting to keep certain direct combat positions, such as infantry and machinegunner, closed to women. "There will be no exceptions," Secretary Carter said at a news conference. "They'll be allowed to drive tanks, fire mortars, and lead infantry soldiers into combat. They'll be able to serve as Army Rangers and Green Berets, Navy SEALs, Marine Corps infantry, Air Force parajumpers, and everything else that was previously open only to men." Secretary Carter asserted that combat fitness standards will not be lowered, to fill the job a woman will have to meet the same qualifications as a male aspirant. Finally, in April 2016 the House Armed Services Committee approved legislation known as the "Draft America's Daughters Act of 2016." If this measure is passed into law, young women between the ages of eighteen to twenty-six will inherit military service obligations the same as for men.

Welcome to combat, ladies.

WRIGHT BROTHERS

{ On December 17, 1903, Orville Wright piloted the first powered airplane over the beach at Kitty Hawk, North Carolina. That one flight changed the history of travel.
Well, not really. }

What history seems to have forgotten is that the flight wasn't an idiosyncratic event, not the only flight that morning. It was one of four achieved that day, each surpassing the accomplishment of the previous one. That first, at 10:35 a.m., lasted twelve seconds and covered 120 feet at a speed of 6.8 miles per hour. Orville's brother Wilbur piloted the second flight, which extended 175 feet, followed by Orville at the controls for the third, covering 200 feet.

At about noon Wilbur performed the final and longest flight of the day. For the first few hundred feet the plane performed unevenly, then settled in to a well-controlled path for about 400 to 500 feet until it became irregular once again and hit the ground after fifty-nine seconds, having flown 852 feet. That was it for the day, the plane slightly damaged. Later that afternoon, the plane was damaged more severely by wind and never flown again.

Several years later Orville restored the plane and it eventually made its way to the Smithsonian Museum in DC, where it is still on display. Simply named *The Flyer*, the 605-pound craft is 21.1 feet long and has a 40.3 foot wingspan. The 170-pound, four-cylinder twelve-horsepower engine sits on the right side of the centerline and the pilots, weighing 145 pounds, lay on the left side. For balance, the right wing was made four inches longer to produce slightly more lift than the left.

Though not claiming to be the first flight, the Wright brothers are credited with making the first power-driven, controlled, and sustained heavier-than-air flight.

NERO AND THE BURNING OF ROME

{ Nero has become infamous for playing his fiddle while Rome burned.
Don't you believe it. }

Nero wasn't in Rome when the great fire broke out. He was lazing at his summer home in Antium (the current Anzio), some thirty-five miles away. According to the Roman historian Tacitus, when the fire erupted, on July 18 in the year AD 64, Nero returned to Rome and instituted measures to limit the damage, organized facilities for those affected, and provided food and accommodations for the victims.

The fire burned for six days and seven nights, consuming 70 percent of the city, totally destroying three of Rome's fourteen districts, severely damaging seven others. Among the areas demolished were the slopes of the Palatine hill, which contained the stately homes of the Roman gentry. When the conflagration had burned itself out, the word spread that Nero had started it in order to clear ground to create a new city of his own design, built around his Domus Aurea, an immense planned palace with 300 rooms but no sleeping facilities, intended as a center for entertainment. The rumor was credible because Nero was known to preside at numerous parties and banquets. To deflect the Romans' suspicions, he blamed the devastation on the growing faction of Christians, and initiated a reign of arrests and executions, providing the empire's first period of persecution against them.

But today's historians doubt his guilt. In spite of his murderous reputation, having had his mother and two wives killed, the evidence does not support his pyromania. The fire originated a full kilometer from the site to be the Domus, and his own villa was badly damaged by the fire.

Besides, Nero couldn't have played the fiddle; it wasn't to be invented until several centuries later. Nero's instrument was the lyre.

LIGHTNING

{ Lightning never strikes twice in the same place.
Don't you believe it. }

Lightning frequently strikes twice in the same place, unless cloud or ground conditions have changed significantly. Lightning is "a sudden electrostatic discharge during an electrical storm between electrically charged regions of a cloud (called intra-cloud lightning, or IC), between that cloud and another cloud (CC lightning), or between a cloud and the ground (CG lightning)." Lightning, then, is an electrical discharge between positive and negative zones of a thunderstorm. But the concentration of electrical particles remains fairly constant over a short period of time, so the conditions promoting lightning remain.

A lightning flash is really a series of spasms, about four on average. The duration of each spasm can vary, but usually lasts about thirty microseconds. Collectively, the spasms add up to a flash. IC lightning is the most common type, but the CG type is the one that concerns us here.

Lightning strikes several million times a year in the US, mostly in the summer. Records indicate that lightning kills about fifty people a year in the US and injures hundreds more, some severely. Many people make the mistake of trying to take refuge under a tree, one of the worst places to be when lightning strikes. A tree, being relatively tall in reference to its surroundings, will attract the lightning and pass off the electricity to a person standing under it. It is safer to get indoors where the plumbing lines and water pipes will be better conductors of the electricity to the ground.

Though others had previously observed that lightning resembled sparking, it was Ben Franklin who experimentally demonstrated that lightning was an electrical phenomenon.

TRAFFIC JAMS

{ Southern California, especially the Los Angeles area, is known for its traffic jams, possibly the world's worst. **Don't you believe it.** }

Several places have witnessed worse traffic jams. One of the worst was the well documented three-day tie-up on the New York Thruway, August 15–18, 1969, accompanying the historic Woodstock Music and Arts Festival on Max Yasgur's farm in Bethel, New York. The half million attendees, ten times the amount anticipated, clogged the Thruway for more than twenty miles. Several motorists abandoned their cars and trudged to the event on foot.

Among other notable shutdowns:

Chicago, February 1, 2011. A blizzard during the evening rush hour dropped over twenty inches of snow, burying cars up their windshields. Aggravated by weather-related accidents, the inclemency closed roads for over twelve hours.

Germany, April 12, 1990. The Berlin Wall between the East and West now gone, the Easter holiday promised the opportunity to spend time with family and rekindle old friendships, and the eighteen million cars attempting to do so caused a record-breaking backup on roads not constructed to handle that much traffic.

Houston, Texas, September 21, 2005. Advised to clear out before Hurricane Rita arrived, two-and-a-half million residents clogged evacuation routes, locking up one hundred miles of Interstate 45 for forty-eight hours.

But the worst closure on record occurred in Beijing, China, in August 2010, when sixty-two miles of the Beijing-Tibet expressway jammed up and didn't clear for an unbelievable twelve days. For some travelers, the sixty-two-mile trip took three days. No disaster was to blame, simply too many cars on the road, including heavy trucks ironically carrying construction supplies intended for road repairs that would move traffic more efficiently.

BRITAIN'S FIRST AMERICAN COLONY

{ The Pilgrim colony at Plymouth, Massachusetts, was the first English settlement in America. **Don't you believe it.** }

Thirty-seven years earlier, in the summer of 1584, the Roanoke Colony was founded by Walter Raleigh in present-day North Carolina. Queen Elizabeth's charter called for Raleigh to establish a colony and a base for privateers to prey on Spanish ships for the treasure they carried. The point was to warn Spain that England was prepared for war. Sir Francis Drake visited the colony in 1586, having fought the Spanish in St. Augustine, and he took the surviving settlers back to England but left fifteen men to manage their fort. When a second group of settlers arrived in 1587 they came upon an uninhabited area, but left 117 new colonists, men, women, and children. In August 1590, a supply ship found the colony deserted. No one knows what happened to the colonists and the settlement came to be known as "the lost colony." But it was the first.

Then, in May 1607, a group of about 100 men (no women or children) of the Virginia Company established a settlement on the banks of the James River in Virginia. They named it Jamestown, and it became the first permanent English settlement in North America. The initial two years were severely strained by disease, conflict with local tribes, and a shortage of food. Most of the colonists were unskilled English gentlemen who had no understanding of farming. They had come in search of gold and to find a connection to the Pacific Ocean to provide a passage for trade. Within a few months, about half their number had died. The community was saved by the 1610 arrival of a new batch of settlers and a supply of necessities. They were also saved by tobacco, which they grew and sold to England in vast quantities.

So Plymouth was actually the third.

FULTON'S STEAMBOAT

{ Robert Fulton, American engineer, inventor, and painter created the first steamboat in 1807 which he named the *Clermont*.
Don't you believe it. }

This statement is doubly wrong. More significantly, Fulton did not invent the steamboat. Boats at the time were the major carriers for moving cargo along the Southern rivers. Running with the current was easy, but returning by poling a boat upriver was not. A new energy source for moving river craft would be extremely valuable. Several early attempts had been made to develop a boat powered by steam, the first patents issued in England in 1729 and 1736; but neither produced an operable craft.

After James Watt produced a sophisticated steam-powered engine in 1769, inventors everywhere began trying to adapt it to power boats. In 1783 the first steam-powered vessel, the paddle-boat *Pyroscaphe*, was built in France by Marquis Claude de Jouffroy. On its test run it operated for about fifteen minutes before its engine failed. The first functional steamboat in America was built by John Fitch in 1787 for use on the Delaware River. Capable of carrying thirty passengers, it was successful for a while but scuttled by its high operating costs. Fulton constructed his steamboat learning partly from Fitch's mistakes and on August 17, 1807, it made its 150-mile maiden voyage New York to Albany in thirty-two hours. Beginning in September it was making regular runs every four days between the two cities, carrying as many as one hundred passengers. Fulton had found a way make steam powered boats commercially feasible; and the age of steamboats was initiated.

Second, Fulton didn't name his boat *Clermont*; he called it *North River Steamboat*, as North River the early name of the Hudson River. The name *Clermont* first appeared in a biography of Fulton two years after his death.

The Flag on Mount Surabachi

{ One of the most famous photos from World War II shows several servicemen raising an American flag on the heights of Mount Suribachi after the US marines secured the Pacific island of Iwo Jima from the Japanese Imperial forces.
Don't you believe it. }

The photo was posed, faked for the event. It did not record the smaller flag that had been raised earlier when the Marines first secured the top of the hill, a flag that had been carried by one of the servicemen to be displayed as a symbol of the US Marines' victory over the Japanese defenders.

But that smaller flag was not impressive enough, its presentation not sufficiently eloquent, so the event was restaged more theatrically in the presence of photographer Joe Rosenthal. His photo, taken on February 23, 1945, became an iconic emblem of American military strength and the brotherhood of its fighting men. It was the only photograph to win the Pulitzer Prize for Photography in the same year as its publication.

The battle of Iwo Jima provided one of the pivotal victories of the American campaign in the Pacific theatre of operations. The American invasion, designated Operation Detachment, was intended to capture the Japanese airfields on the island to provide a base for bombing runs on the Japanese mainland, at half the distance from the Mariana Islands where the air force attacks had previously originated. Controlling the island would also remove the Japanese fighter presence that hindered the flights from the Marianas.

Of the six men in the photo, three did not survive the operation, but the three that did became celebrities. The photo became the model for the Marine Corps War Memorial at the Arlington National Cemetery.

US MINTS

{ The United States Mint produces coins in three locations: Philadelphia, Denver, and San Francisco. All others that had operated in the past are now closed. **Don't you believe it.** }

The coins in circulation today are produced at Philadelphia and Denver. The San Francisco mint, until 1975 a source of circulating coins, thereafter produced only proof coins for collectors and the Susan B. Anthony dollar.

Philadelphia is the country's oldest mint, having operated continuously since its founding in 1793. The Denver mint has been in operation since 1863, but producing coins only since 1906; before that it functioned as an assay office testing ore mined in the area.

Hardly known is the branch of the mint that operates at West Point in New York State. Here are minted gold, silver, and platinum bullion coins, and commemoratives as authorized by Congress, for example the one-ounce American Buffalo Gold Bullion Coin. West Point also functions as a storehouse for bullion of all three precious metals. The remaining active division of the mint is Fort Knox in Kentucky, where most of the country's gold bullion is stored. There is no manufacturing at Ft. Knox; it is solely a repository.

And there have been several other branches that no longer operate. From 1838 to 1861 gold coins were minted in Charlotte, North Carolina, and Dahlonega, Georgia; from 1838 to 1909 gold and silver coins were produced at New Orleans, with a break from 1861 to 1879 during the Civil War and Reconstruction; a mint at Carson City, Nevada, produced circulating coins from 1870 to 1893, inactive from 1885 to 1889.

But perhaps the least known facility was at Manila in the Philippines from 1920 to 1922 and 1925 to 1941 that minted centavos for local distribution.

THE LIBERTY BELL

> The bell in the tower of the Pennsylvania State House (later renamed Independence Hall) was rung on July 8, 1776, summoning the citizens of Philadelphia to gather in order to hear the first reading of the Declaration of Independence.
> **Don't you believe it.**

It never happened.

The bell was installed on March 10, 1753, but cracked on its first test ring. Two local metalworkers melted down the bell and cast a replacement, keeping its original inscription from Leviticus, "Proclaim LIBERTY throughout all the Land unto all the Inhabitants thereof."

The sound of the new bell was still unsatisfactory. It was then melted down once again, recast a second time, and rehung in the belfry during the first week in June 1753, the sound still disappointing.

Nevertheless, it did toll several events: when King George III ascended to the throne in 1761, when the Sugar Act was instituted in 1764, and again for the Stamp Act in 1765. But did it ring on July 8, 1776? No one knows for sure, but there are no accounts or newspaper articles from the period confirming that it did. Historians generally think it did not.

It wasn't until the 1830s that the bell achieved its symbolic status, when abolitionists embraced it as an emblem of their crusade. Its likeness appeared on publications of the New York Anti-Slavery Society, when the abolitionists designated it "Liberty Bell," solemnizing the epitaph inscribed on it.

It is uncertain when the crack began on the rebuilt bell, but it is known that the injury had progressed enough to make the bell unringable by Washington's Birthday in 1846.

So it appears that the Liberty Bell celebrated the liberty of ex-slaves from their masters, not the liberty of the colonists from their English rulers.

THE IRS

{
The government's Internal Revenue Service, which bears the responsibility for handling much of our money, can be trusted to manage it responsibly. **Don't you believe it.**
}

In his marvelous book, *The Natural History of Stupidity*, author Paul Tabori tells of one man's experience with the incompetence of the bureaucratic IRS, which he equates with a Kafka story. The man in question, while monitoring his finances, discovered that he had overpaid his previous year's income tax by $72 and in fear of some undefined retribution he asked for that amount to be credited to his current year's tax. Within the month he received a government refund check for that exact amount. This seemed to put the matter to rest and he proceeded to deposit the check and let the incident escape from his thoughts.

Later, along with the bill for the second installment of his estimated tax, he received a report informing him that his overpayment of last year's tax would be credited toward the current year's tax, as he had requested. This still left him in possession of $72 that he considered to be of the government's money and the increased certainly that he was at risk for indictment for something beyond his control. To forestall a dreaded legal action against him, and being basically an honest sort of fellow, he wrote to the Collector of Internal Revenue recounting the details of his present plight and seeking a way to resolve the problem.

The official agency response left him questioning the government's collective sanity: "Dear Sir," it began, "When your tax return is audited, your request for a credit of $72 on your current tax for overpayment on your previous year's tax will almost certainly be disallowed."

And you think your accounts are screwed up!

CIVIL WAR GENERALS

> The Union army in the Civil War had an advantage over the Confederate forces because many Union generals had received formal training in warfare from the government's Military Academy at West Point. **Yes, but . . .**

True, a large proportion of Union officers were products of the West Point, but so were many of the Southern commanders, who had also graduated from West Point and served with the Union army before joining the grays.

When an interim Confederate Congress authorized a provisional volunteer army on February 28, 1861, Union officers were painfully confronted with deciding where to assign their loyalty—to remain with the Federals or return to their states. Many regular officers felt they could not betray their home state and they chose to resign their commission and join their state militia, all of which of course later became part of the Confederate military.

According to official US Army military records, when the war began the American "regular army" had 1,080 commissioned officers, 824 of them graduates of West Point; 286 resigned or were dismissed and joined the Confederacy; 184 of those had attended the Academy. Other than graduates then in military service, approximately 900 others were in civilian life; 114 returned to the Union army and ninety-nine others joined the Confederacy. So the count were not quite as disparate as might be expected.

This explains why so many Northern commanders were familiar with their Southern counterparts. They had earlier been assigned to the same stations. They had fought in the same battles. Many had served together in the Mexican War some fifteen years earlier. In addition, more than a few families had officers in both the Union and Confederate armies.

GEORGE WASHINGTON FOR PRESIDENT

{ Following his service in the Revolutionary War, Washington coveted the presidency. **Don't you believe it.** }

In truth, Washington wasn't sure he wanted to be president. His letters and diaries reveal that he was unsure of his abilities and ridden by self-doubt. Perhaps more than any other reason, he was worried that the exemplary reputation he had earned as leader of the Revolutionary Army might be damaged by missteps in the role of president of the new republic. Above all, he craved returning to Mount Vernon, his Virginia plantation, to live out his days peacefully. He wrote to Benjamin Lincoln, an army comrade, that if he were pressured to undertake the presidency, which "would be the greatest sacrifice to my personal feelings & wishes that ever I have been called upon to make. It would be to forego repose and domestic enjoyment; for trouble, perhaps; for public obloquy; for I should consider myself as entering upon an unexplored field, enveloped on every side with clouds & darkness."

But his friends refused to accept his insecurity. The Marquis de Lafayette wrote to him, "in the Name of America, of Mankind at Large, and Your Own fame, I beseech you, my dear General, Not to deny your Acceptance of the office of president." Harry Lee Jr., another army comrade, saw him as offering the best potential for uniting the separate colonies into a unified nation. "Without you," Lee wrote, "the govt can have but little chance of success."

And so he consented. But he began his inaugural address by confessing that "no event could have filled me with greater anxieties" than accepting the office of the president, and that, mindful of his "deficiencies," how could he not be overwhelmed with "despondence"?

History records his performance as the first president.

COWBOYS

{ Cowboys had a great life: freedom, independence, living close to nature in the open air.
Don't you believe it. }

The cowboys' life was nowhere near as attractive as is portrayed in Hollywood westerns. The job was dangerous, dirty, repetitive, and generally pretty dull. Their workday could run to fifteen hours, mostly in the saddle, prodding, coaxing, and herding large-sized beasts over long distances. A cattle drive averaged two to three months, from the grassy plains to railway towns where the animals would be loaded onto stock cars and shipped to big city abattoirs to be slaughtered and prepared for the dining table.

On the trail, riding amid and around 1,500-pound longhorn cattle could be daunting. Worse yet if the drivers lost command of the throng and the animals stampeded. Working to control the mass could be extremely perilous; one error or miscalculation could easily lead to serious injury, even death.

Cowboys were largely young, uneducated, and unprepared for any other employment. Many had lost their parents and friends in the Civil War and had no support system to turn to for help. The job was often the only available source of any income in a world of desperation. For some it was an excitement, for many more it was subsistence, not at all the glamorous life portrayed in escapist fiction. The open-range era lasted from around 1866 to 1886.

The romantic image of the brave cowboy is the creation of trashy novels and fatuous films that have little authenticity. A more accurate portrayal of cowboys would show them living among rattlesnakes, aggressive prairie vermin, and other wildlife, not to mention frequently lousy weather and, of course, a variety of hostile Indian tribes.

It's no wonder that only one of three cowboys returned for another drive.

The First World War

{
The June 1914 killing of Archduke Franz Ferdinand,
heir to the throne of the Austro-Hungarian Empire,
by a young Serbian nationalist in Sarajevo, Bosnia,
incited the first World War.
Don't you believe it.
}

The assassination of the Archduke was the *causa proxima* of the Great War that involved a good part of the world from July 1914 to November 1918. But that global conflict was not the first of such inclusiveness as to be termed a *world war*.

That distinction, according to many historians, should be accorded to the Seven Years' War of 1756 to 1763, primarily a struggle between the British Empire and France but involving a great number of the world's nations and fought over an unprecedented worldwide scope. The North American component of that conflict is what we know as the French and Indian War.

The Seven Years' War pitted France, Austria, Russia, Sweden, and Saxony, joined by Spain after 1762, against Prussia, England, and Hanover. Two main contentions fueled the enmity: French-English rivalry in expanding their colonial empires in America and India, and the struggle for domination of Germany between Maria Teresa of Austria and Frederick II of Prussia. The advantage in the latter engagement fluctuated back and forth until Peter III took control of Russia and negotiated a separate peace with Frederick, while England under the leadership of William Pitt secured victories in several venues.

The Seven Years' War, regarded as perhaps the first true World War, almost 160 years before World War I, was ended by the Treaty of Hubertusburg and the Treaty of Paris. The first established Russia's status as an international player; the second confirmed England's prominence over France as the world's primary colonial power.

INVENTING CHAMPAGNE

{ It is well known that champagne was invented by
Dom Perignon, a Benedictine monk, in about 1697.
Don't you believe it. }

Well known, but not true. Dom Perignon did not invent champagne.

The first sparkling wine dates from 1531, made by Benedictine monks at the Abbey of Saint-Hilaire near Carcassonne, France more than 150 years before Dom Perignon. They achieved the bubbly by bottling the wine before the fermentation was complete.

Sparkling wine is created when a second fermentation occurs in a closed bottle. Before the process was understood, wine bottles were filled in autumn, before weather turned cool and interrupted fermentation, and often exploded in storage when the temperature rose in the spring. The increase in warmth revived the wine's dormant yeast to produce carbon dioxide bubbles in secondary fermentation.

In 1662 a British scientist, Christopher Merret, presented a paper to the Royal Society detailing a "second fermentation process" in which sugar and molasses are added to wines to make them "drink brisk and sparkling." This pretty well matches the *methode champenoise*, the way champagne is now made. He described a chemical reaction in which bottled alcohol responds to a rise in temperature and induces carbonization.

Dom Perignon was cellar master at the Benedictine abbey in Hautvillers in northeastern France. Among his contributions to wine-making, he was the first to improve quality by blending grapes, he knew how to time bottling for best results, and he knew how to control the way Champagne wines preserved their natural sugar to induce secondary fermentation in the spring.

But he didn't invent champagne. In fact, early on he tried to prevent secondary fermentation, which was thought a fault of wine-making.

Besides, it looks like Champagne might really have been a British invention.

THE DEATH OF DIANA

{ Princess Diana died in an auto crash, caused by over-zealous paparazzi trailing hers in other vehicles. **Don't you believe it.** }

In July 1981, Lady Diana Spencer wed Prince Charles, heir to the throne of England. Affectionately known as Princess Di, she became the darling of the English people: she was young, attractive, and brought vitality to the otherwise stodgy British royal family. The marriage was not happy but it produced two sons and was maintained for propriety's sake. Meanwhile, Diana had a five-year affair beginning in 1986 with her sons' riding instructor, Major James Hewitt. She and Charles separated in December 1992, and divorced in August 1996.

Following her divorce, Diana retained a high level of popularity. She devoted herself to her sons and to her charitable endeavors, staying in the public eye through reports of her relationships with several men. But in 1997, she found the man she considered her true love—playboy Dodi Fayed, owner of Harrods Department Store in London. On holiday in Paris, just after midnight on August 31, 1997, Diana and Dodi left the Ritz Hotel in a black Mercedes followed by a clutch of photographers. Driver Henri Paul was able to outrun most of them, but in an underpass at the Pont de l'Alma, driving over 100 miles per hour, he crashed into a concrete post, killing himself and Dodi and sending Diana to the hospital in critical condition, where she later died.

A French investigation concluded that the paparazzi were distant from the Mercedes and were not responsible, but "the driver of the car was inebriated . . . not in a position to maintain control of the vehicle." A British inquest also attributed the accident to gross negligence by driver Henri Paul, who was found to have a blood alcohol level three times the legal limit. The paparazzi were exonerated.

HAMILTON AND BURR

> Alexander Hamilton and Aaron Burr, who faced off against each other in what was probably the most famous duel in American history, were lifelong adversaries.
> **Don't you believe it.**

Hamilton and Burr were both lawyers, frequently on opposite sides in legal actions. They were also political opponents. Hamilton is quoted as observing that they "had always been opposed on politics but always in good terms." Others in their circle did not see them as quite so conciliatory. But there was one trial that had them working together as co-counsels.

It is remembered as the Manhattan Well Murder case of 1800 in New York; incidentally it is the first murder trial in the United States for which a recorded transcript exists. A young man named Levi Weeks was accused of killing Gulielma Sands, a young woman he had been dating. She disappeared on December 22, 1799; her body was found in a nearby well, from which it was recovered eleven days later. Before leaving her boarding house on the night she disappeared, Gulielma had told her cousin she was planning to elope with Levi Weeks that evening.

Through his influential brother's connections, Weeks retained Aaron Burr and Alexander Hamilton, two prominent attorneys, to defend him. Ezra Weeks was a wealthy contractor who had Burr and Hamilton as clients. Both were in debt to Ezra and he called in those favors. But Hamilton and Burr were commercial lawyers, neither having had much contact with murder cases before, so they took on a third attorney, an experienced criminal lawyer named Henry Brockholst Livingston. The trial lasted two days, the jury's deliberation only five minutes to acquit Weeks.

So at least on one occasion Hamilton and Burr had worked together as co-counsels on the same side only four years before their historic duel.

HELEN KELLER

We all learned about Helen Keller in school. That a childhood disease left her blind and deaf at the age of nineteen months, and how dedicated teacher Anne Sullivan helped her overcome her physical handicaps, taught her to communicate, and helped her develop her true potential. But we know almost nothing about her complex adult life.

You can believe it.

Helen Keller has been appropriated as the confirmation that no person is incapable of being helped. Her story of childhood struggle has been inspirational for many generations of both children and adults. Several movies have been created about her, but her later life is not discussed. The reason is simple: The details of her adult life do not provide a comfortable portrait for inclusion in the pantheon of American heroes.

Americans seem embarrassed to learn that she was a radical socialist, becoming a member of the Socialist party of Massachusetts in 1906. She glorified the new communist nation created by the Russian Revolution. She was an early and stout supporter of Socialist Eugene V. Debs in his several candidacies for the presidency. She spoke out for and demonstrated for women's suffrage. And she helped found the American Civil Liberties Union to safeguard free speech, which she honored, having struggled so hard to attain for herself the ability to speak.

At the time she joined the Socialist Party she was among the most esteemed women alive. But soon she became one of the most vilified. Her radicalism did not go down well with the media or with the public at large. So she was excluded from the limelight, deposed from her pedestal, and pretty well lost from view.

But she does prove to be a more controversial and interesting person than the one we thought we knew.

THE CHICAGO FIRE

{
On the night of October 8, 1871, a great fire broke out in Chicago, reputedly started when a cow owned by Mrs. Catherine O'Leary kicked over a lamp in her barn on DeKoven Street.
Don't you believe it.
}

The Chicago fire started at about 9 p.m. in the vicinity of the O'Leary barn. Before burning out two days later, it had destroyed over 3.3 square miles of the city, leaving several hundred dead, 100,000 homeless, and property damage of close to $200 million. It destroyed the downtown business area and the North Side, but it was less damaging to the stockyards and lumberyards on the South and West Sides. Misdirected fire equipment arrived too late, and a determined southwesterly wind carried the flames and burning debris across the city.

The cause of the fire was never established. It could have been a careless neighbor, a thief, pranksters, but not likely a malevolent cow. The blaze was supported by the parched condition of the city, having recorded barely any rain since early July, and by the city's predilection for houses of wood, most topped with highly combustible tar or shingle roofs. Sidewalks were also made of wood. Almost two dozen fires had erupted within two weeks before the big one. The O'Leary's barn burned down but, oddly enough, their home escaped the flames when the wind changed direction.

But the cow story caught on, fueled by the anti-Irish bias then endemic to Chicago. Several decades later, in a Chicago Tribune article, reporter Michael Ahern admitted that he and a few other newsmen had created the cow story to add color to an article they had written. A reporter had heard such a tale from nearby residents and the paper had run it without confirmation.

The fire did have a salutary effect: rebuilding brought in leading architects and workmen who created America's first modern city and introduced skyscrapers. Chicago's population at the time of the fire was about 325,000; some twenty-five years later, as a major industrial and transportation center, it had grown to an estimated 1.5 million people.

In 1955, the city built a new Chicago Fire Academy on the site of the O'Leary's barn.

In 1997, the Chicago City Council voted to exonerate Catherine O'Leary, and her cow.

The Chicago fire achieved international fame, but in doing so it overshadowed an even bigger conflagration, and thus the worst recorded forest fire in North American history was consigned to obscurity. The fire, centered in Peshtigo, Wisconsin—250 miles due north of Chicago—began earlier in the same day as the Chicago fire, destroying millions of dollars of forestland and other property, and causing the most deaths by fire in United States history, estimated between 1,500 and 2,500. (A firm count is impossible because this frontier settlement had a number of itinerant lumber workers and immigrant settlers.) Before it ended the fire devoured almost 1,900 square miles of forest and consumed twelve communities.

The whole north-central part of the country was in the throes of a dry spell, rain and snowfall had been sparse, the land was parched with logs, debris, and sawdust from the lumber mills piled everywhere. The entire north woods were bone dry and finally the tinderbox ignited and developed into a firestorm. There was no fire department in the area so bucket brigades were the fire-fighting norm. People headed for the bridge, which seemed a safe area. The bridge caught fire. The blaze crossed the river and burned on, ravaging both sides. To escape the flames people plunged into the Peshtigo River. Some drowned, while others suffered hypothermia in the icy water. By midnight the fire had burned itself out. Looting and other violations were common and martial law was declared on October 11.

But the Chicago fire is better known because it occupied a bustling city; Peshtigo was only a frontier settlement.

THE LIGHT BULB

{
Everyone knows that Thomas Edison invented the incandescent light bulb.
Don't you believe it.
}

The incandescent bulb was not, in the usual sense, invented by Edison. Although Edison patented the first commercially practical incandescent bulb in 1879, he was only one of many contributors to its development. Incandescence results from electrically heating a wire filament until it glows with visible light. Oxidation of the heated filament is prevented by enclosure in a protective glass bulb filled with either a vacuum or an inert gas.

In 1802, English inventor Humphrey Davy connected charcoal electrodes to voltaic piles, creating an electric arc lamp. But the light produced was too bright for practical use. At the beginning of the 1840s two British inventors, Warren de la Rue and Frederick de Moleyns, independently tried platinum filaments in a vacuum, but both found platinum too expensive to commercialize. In 1851, Joseph Wilson Swan, a British physicist, used a carbonized paper filament, but technology of the time could not produce an adequate vacuum in its bulb. In 1874, Canadian Henry Woodward and co-worker Mathew Evans tried carbon rods in nitrogen, but they too were unable to commercialize their lamp.

Meanwhile, in 1865, the invention of the mercury pump facilitated the creation of a better vacuum, which Swan utilized in 1878 to produce a satisfactory light bulb. Edison's, using carbonized bamboo, was developed the following year.

By 1880, both Swan and Edison applied for patents and litigation ensued. It was resolved when they formed a joint company in 1883. In the popular mind, however, Edison was credited with the invention because he developed the power lines and other equipment needed to build a practical lighting system using the incandescent lamp.

OTHER QUICK ONES

The Nazis didn't start the Reichstag fire in February 1933; it was set by a Dutch socialist, Marinus van der Lubbe, protesting Nazism. Lubbe was caught, confessed, and found guilty at what appeared a fair trial. He was beheaded. But the Nazis used the event to blame the communists.

General Ulysses S. Grant (later President Grant) was known to quail in the presence of blood. Which sounds like a serious hindrance for a battlefield commander. If his dinner contained a cut of meat, it had to be very well done or charred.

The tomato is a fruit, not a vegetable, although in 1893 the US Supreme Court ruled it a vegetable. But the Court's ruling was based on how we eat it, not on its biology. Their ruling observed that it is "usually served at dinner in, with, or after the soup, fish, or meat . . . and not, like the fruits generally, as dessert." Nonetheless, biologically a fruit contains seeds and develops from the ovary of a plant, while a vegetable is a different part of the plant, such as a tuber for a potato of the leaves for lettuce.

We are told that cats always land on their feet, no matter how far they fall or their position when dropped. Not true. Cats can be seriously injured in falls from high places.

Van Gogh did not aspire to be an artist. His ambition was the priesthood, but he was denied entrance to several theology schools when he failed the entrance exams. Finally placed as a missionary in a Belgian village, he was let go after eight months for being overzealous. Then he took up painting.

There never was a Dutch boy who prevented a flood by sticking his finger in a dike. That character was created by Mary Mapes Dodge, an American author, in her book *Hans Brinker, or the Silver Skates*.

Neville Chamberlain got a bad rap when he returned from Munich in 1938, committing Great Britain to a course of appeasement and not resisting Germany's takeover of Czechoslovakia. Later evidence indicated that Britain was not militarily prepared to confront Hitler at that stage.

GENERAL PATTON ON D-DAY

{ General George Patton, one of the American army's most effective commanders, had a pivotal role in the D-Day invasion of the European continent. **Don't you believe it.** }

General George Patton had made a name for himself early in the war commanding Allied forces in North Africa and again in the invasion of Sicily. But Patton had become a public relations liability and he was relieved of his last command. He was nonetheless a natural choice to lead the invasion of Europe, and the Germany military expected him to do so.

General Eisenhower, supreme commander of the upcoming European invasion, played into that expectation to deceive the Germans. Eisenhower put Patton in command of the newly established First US Army Group (FUSAG), a fictitious force meant to convince the Germans that the invasion would occur in the Pas de Calais area. The deception, designated Operation Quicksilver, purported a million-man army stationed at Dover, evidenced by fields of tents, dozens of fake inflatable tanks, artillery, trucks, and even aircraft, all of which appeared real to observation planes. Abundant radio communications were created and local inlets filled with fleets of dummy landing boats. This massive force demanded a seasoned battle commander to make the operation credible to the Germans. Patton had the ideal image for the position; he was well-known to the Germans as a tough offensive warrior.

The phantom army was one of the largest and most elaborate—and, as it turned out, effective—deceptions in the history of warfare. The Germans concentrated defensive forces at Pas de Calais, and the Allied invasion at Normandy was a celebrated success.

Later, Patton did see service on the continent; he distinguished himself as commander of the Third Army.

BOMBING CIVILIANS

{ Among the charges relating to the Germans' brutality
in the Second World War was their decision to bomb
civilian areas with no military component.
Don't you believe it. }

The bombing of civilians was not inaugurated by the Germans
against the British, but instead by the British against German
cities. Winston Churchill is said to have argued that engaging
civilians would demoralize the German population and destroy
their will to fight. The British began bombing German civilians
in the Ruhr as early as May 15–16, 1940.

The German's concentrated bombing of London, widely
known as the Blitz, didn't begin until September 7, 1940, and for
fifty-seven consecutive days hammered the city, day and night.
The raids continued until May 21, 1941 when Hitler withdrew
his bombers in his buildup of forces to attack Russia.

Of course, the official word blamed the Nazis for bringing
the war to civilians. Respected British historian J. F. P. Veale has
observed, "It is one of the greatest triumphs of modern emotional
engineering that, in spite of the plain facts of the case which could
never be disguised or even materially distorted, the British public,
throughout the Blitz Period, remained convinced that the entire
responsibility for their suffering rested on the German leaders."

Germany had already bombed civilian targets in Poland
but seemed to delay hitting civilian London until after France
surrendered on June 22. Both sides had previously bombed the
enemy's military targets, but records indicate that the first British
noncombatant bombing deaths occurred when a German aircraft
lost its way over London and mistakenly dropped its explosives on
several houses instead of factories, killing civilians.

So it seems that the Germans did it first—but accidently. The
British did it first very much intentionally.

SECESSION

{
The southern states seceded from the Union to preserve states' rights, not because of slavery. **Don't you believe it.**
}

Their own documents contradict this. Four of the seven states that initially seceded had each prepared a *Declaration of Causes*, all clear in the centrality of slavery to their decision. Mississippi's, for example, was short and explicit: "Our position is thoroughly identified with the institution of slavery . . . a blow at slavery is a blow at commerce and civilization."

Georgia: "The North demanded the application of the principle of prohibition of slavery . . . her fixed purpose to limit, restrain, and finally abolish slavery in the States where it exists . . . the equality of the black and white races were boldly proclaimed by its leaders and applauded by its followers."

South Carolina: "[Lincoln's] opinions and purposes are hostile to slavery . . . he has declared that 'Government cannot endure permanently half slave, half free,' and . . . that a war must be waged against slavery until it shall cease throughout the United States."

Texas: "We hold as undeniable truths that the governments of the various States, and of the confederacy itself, were established exclusively by the white race, for themselves and their posterity; that the African race had no agency in their establishment; that they were rightfully held and regarded as an inferior and dependent race. . . . [T]he servitude of the African race . . . is abundantly authorized and justified by the experience of mankind, and the revealed will of the Almighty Creator, as recognized by all Christian nations; while the destruction of the existing relations between the two races, as advocated by our sectional enemies, would bring inevitable calamities upon both and desolation upon the fifteen slave-holding states."

FOREIGN AID

{
The United States' moral and humanitarian leadership of the world is shown by our supremacy among the world's nations in providing foreign aid to those nations that most need it.
Don't you believe it.
}

In 2014, the latest year for which data is available at the time of this writing, the United States donated the most foreign aid of all countries, $32 billion. But that figure is not so impressive when viewed as a percentage of the gross national income (GNI); it is only 0.19 percent, the same as Portugal and Japan. Several other countries contributed a much higher share.

A target of 0.7 percent of GNI had been established as an official development assistance (ODA) by the UN in 1970, that level of ODA/GNI accepted by the twenty-nine members that later signed on to the OECD's Development Assistance Committee (DAC). The EU members that were in the DAC agreed to reach the target by 2015. By 2014, five had succeeded. Sweden led the pack, donating 1.1 percent of its GNI to foreign aid. Luxembourg donated 1.07 percent, Norway 0.99 percent, Denmark 0.85 percent, and the UK 0.71 percent. Among those countries that didn't make the target were Germany at 0.41 percent, France at 0.36 percent, and Switzerland at 0.49 percent, all still significantly more than the US.

But the country that donated the most to foreign aid, measured as a percentage of GNI, was the United Arab Emirates (not in the DAC), which contributed an impressive 1.17 percent.

The picture changes if we include nongovernmental aid. The Hudson Institute, a private think tank, estimates private assistance for 2014 at $71.2 billion. That figure, though, is in dispute by some authorities because it includes $47 billion in foreign individuals' remittances to family members. Excluding that item, private aid comes to $24 billion. Added to governmental foreign aid, that brings the sum of US foreign aid to $56 billion, or 0.34 percent, still not even in the top ten.

RESPONSE TO THE GETTYSBURG ADDRESS

{
Lincoln's 272-word address at the consecration of the Gettysburg cemetery drew cheers from the assembled crowd.
Don't you believe it.
}

No such response. When Lincoln finished his remarks on that 1863 day in Pennsylvania, barely a trace of polite applause was heard from the congregants. They appeared obviously disappointed, perhaps because the speech seemed too short to have any significance. The lack of response led him to believe his speech was "a flat failure," and that he had not satisfied the need to honor the site and the war dead buried there. The *Chicago Times* agreed, reviewing his speech as "silly, flat, and dishwatery." It appeared his address would soon be forgotten.

Lincoln was not the featured speaker that November day. In fact, the request for him to attend was almost an afterthought. The invitation wasn't received until two weeks before the event. He was to deliver a few remarks following the major address by former senator Edward Everett, a well-known orator of lofty eloquence. But Everett's words in his two-hour talk are now all but forgotten and Lincoln's have become one of the most memorable speeches in American history. At the time, no one was impressed, except Everett who wrote to Lincoln the following day, "I should be glad, if I could flatter myself that I came as near to the central idea of the occasion, in two hours, as you did in two minutes." Nor did the speech draw much attention in the following years. It was lost to the public memory until the US Centennial in 1876, when its noteworthiness was reassessed in the context of the war's meaning to the history of the hundred-year-old nation.

The speech has now achieved greater salience than the battle that inspired it.

SECTION TWO:
WHO SAYS SO?

Unlike Lincoln's remarks, several noteworthy quotes, though well remembered, are attributed to the incorrect sources; which may distort the intention of an original passage. Not infrequently the real meaning of a saying or a piece of information is clarified by knowing where it originated. For example, "I just killed 'em" means one thing coming from a comic exiting the stage, something quite different spoken by a Mafia hood, different yet again when said by a biological researcher with a petri dish. And oftentimes the original phrase has been misquoted somewhere along the way, altered either by history or by historians. Quotes are frequently shortened or spiced up, the better to illustrate the point the reteller is making. A minor alteration may cause a major misinterpretation. Such distortions are also included here.

Mark Twain is quoted as remarking, "There are three kinds of lies: lies, damn lies, and statistics." But Twain didn't invent the witticism; he merely quoted it in his autobiography, attributing it to Benjamin Disraeli.

* * *

"These are the times that try men's souls." Usually identified as the words of Thomas Paine from his incendiary 1776 pamphlet, *Common Sense*. This is Paine, but it's not from *Common Sense*. It appeared several months later, in December 1776, in *The Crisis No. 1*, the first in a series of pamphlets collectively called *The American Crisis*.

* * *

Lincoln was supposed to have said, "God must have loved the common man; he made so many of them." But it wasn't Lincoln's aphorism. The line comes from a 1928 book, *Our Presidents*, written by James Morgan.

* * *

John Reed, American journalist and social activist, who wrote *Ten Days That Shook the World* about his firsthand observations in Petrograd (now St. Petersburg) during the Russian Revolution, is credited with the phrase "I have seen the future, and it works." But he never said it. Although it would be in character to have come from Reed, the words actually are those of Lincoln Steffens, the muckraking American reporter, after his return from the Soviet Union in 1919.

* * *

General William Tecumseh Sherman is credited with observing that "War is hell." What he actually told a group of Civil War vets in 1880 was, "There is many a boy here today who looks on war as all glory, but, boys, it is all hell." Sherman, by the way, is also remembered for counseling that "No generality is any damn good. And that includes this one."

* * *

Charles E. Wilson, CEO of General Motors, didn't say, "What's good for General Motors is good for the country." When being vetted by a congressional committee for President Eisenhower's Secretary of Defense, Wilson offered the opinion that "What's good for the country is good for General Motors, and vice-versa." The opposition members of the committee dropped the "vice-versa" and turned the statement around to make it sound an arrogant promotion of G.M. Wilson was confirmed.

* * *

Leo Durocher, the irascible baseball manager, is remembered for declaring, "Nice guys finish last." But he never said quite that. In 1946, as manager of the Brooklyn Dodgers, he was disparaging the New York Giants before a few sports writers. He looked over at the Giants' dugout and observed, "They're the nicest guys in the world! And where are they? In seventh place! Nice guys! I'm not a nice guy—and I'm in first place. The nice guys are all over there, in seventh place." When *Baseball Digest* reprinted the incident, "seventh place" came out "last place." And that caught on. Durocher first denied saying it, then adopted the phrase and even used it as the title of his autobiography.

* * *

William Congreve is the author of, "Music hath charms to soothe savage beast." Except he wrote ". . . .oothe the savage *breast*," not "beast."

* * *

Shakespeare has been incorrectly cited as the originator of more quotations than any other author. He never said many of the things he is said to have said. For example, " 'Tis better to have loved and lost than never to have loved at all." (Actually from Alfred Lord Tennyson's "In Memoriam A. H. H.," a requiem to his departed friend, Arthur H. Hallam); "How do I love thee? Let me count the ways." From *Sonnets from the Portuguese*, by Elizabeth Barrett Browning); "Love is a wonderful, terrible thing." (From *Gabriela, Clove and Cinnamon*, a modernist novel by Spanish writer Jorge Amado); "The less you speak of your greatness, the more shall I think of it." (By Sir Francis Bacon, in *To Sir Edmund Coke*); "All glory comes from daring to begin." (From the Eugene Fitch Ware poem, "James Brown"); "Time is too slow for those who wait, / Too swift for those who fear." (In Henry van Dyke's poem, "Time is"); "I love thee, I love but thee / With a love that shall not die." (From "The Bedouin Song," by Bayard Taylor); "Love to faults is always blind, / Always is to joy inclined." (By William Blake, in "Gnomic Verses").

Moreover, there is no "Gild the lily" in Shakespeare. This is a misquote from *King John*, "To gild refined gold, to paint the lily." Nor do the witches in *Macbeth* chant, "Bubble, bubble, toil and trouble." Their ditty is, "Double, double, toil and trouble." And Hamlet doesn't reminisce, "Alas, poor Yorick! I knew him well." Rather, Hamlet recalls, "I knew him, Horatio—a fellow of infinite jest, of most excellent fancy." Also in Hamlet, Gertrude's affirmation is not, "Methinks the lady doth protest too much," but rather, "The lady doth protest too much, methinks." Lastly, Juliet doesn't tell Romeo, "A rose by any other name smells as sweet." What she does say is, "What's in a name? That which we call a rose by any other word would smell as sweet."

* * *

"A little knowledge is a dangerous thing." Perhaps, but Alexander Pope's cautionary remark in "An Essay on Criticism" is really "A little learning is a dangerous thing."

* * *

Often attributed to either Churchill or Mark Twain, author Jonathan Swift is really the source of the apothegm, "A lie can travel halfway around the world while the truth is putting on its shoes."

* * *

It wasn't Marilyn Monroe who suggested that, "Well-behaved women seldom make history." The observation came from Laurel T. Ulrich, a professor at Harvard University in a 1976 journal article.

* * *

Teddy Roosevelt never suggested, "Walk softly, but carry a big stick." Rather, his advice was to, "Speak softly, but carry a big stick."

* * *

"The only thing necessary for the triumph of evil is for good men to do nothing." It is an observation by British statesman Edmund Burke, but he worded it differently: "When bad men combine, the good must associate, else they will fall one by one, an unpitied sacrifice in a contemptible struggle."

* * *

"There is nothing better for the inside of a man than the outside of a horse." An oft confirmed Ronald Reagan comment, though sometimes attributed to Winston Churchill. In any case, it's not original with either of them. Dr. Cary Grayson, Woodrow Wilson's physician, is known to have made a similar remark: "The outside of a horse is good for the inside of man." But no one knows its exact origin—only that it does appear in a 1906 British book, *Social Silhouettes*.

* * *

Marshal Henri Petain, commander of French forces at Verdun in WWI, is credited with stimulating his poilus' enthusiasm by asserting, "They shall not pass." But it was not he who proclaimed, "*Ils ne passeront pas!*" It was his underling, Robert Georges Nivelle, who was apparently more impassioned than his superior.

* * *

Charles Cotesworth Pinkney, negotiating a commercial treaty with France in 1797, didn't say, "Millions for defense, but not one cent for tribute." When pressed to pay a bribe to French agents, he replied, "No! Not a sixpence!" The alleged response was created later by Virginia Congressman Robert Goodloe Harper.

* * *

Isaac Newton, the great English scientist of the seventeenth century, in a rare display of humility, attributed his extraordinary corpus of insights and discoveries to his historical context. In a letter to fellow scientist Robert Hooke he wrote, "If I have seen further, it is by standing on the shoulders of giants." A modest appraisal of his intellectual contributions, but not an original one. His self-effacing assessment has a precedent traceable to the twelfth-century French philosopher Bernard of Chartres.

* * *

"Too many people nowadays know the price of everything and the value of nothing," is traditionally an aphorism usually ascribed to nineteenth-century writer-philosopher Elbert Hubbard. Actually, Oscar Wilde said it earlier, almost verbatim.

* * *

Dr. Seuss, the marvelous writer of children's books, is credited with this observation: "Those who mind don't matter, and those who matter don't mind." Nice homespun philosophizing, but not by Dr. Seuss. It was part of an answer presidential advisor Bernard Baruch gave to a reporter who asked him how he arranged the seating of important people at his dinner parties.

* * *

In 1935, Douglas MacArthur is reported to have stated his opinion: "Only those are fit to live who are not afraid to die." But it is only a restatement of what Theodore Roosevelt wrote a decade earlier: "Only those are fit to live who do not fear to die."

* * *

In his first inaugural address in March 1933, FDR strove to allay the citizenry's foreboding about the uncertain times ahead with his uplifting observation, "All we have to fear is fear itself." Soothing perhaps, but not novel. The same thought had been voiced before, several times. Examples: "The thing of which I have most fear is fear," from Montaigne's *Essays* I, xvii; or "The only thing I am afraid of is fear," from *The Duke of Wellington's Conversations* by Philip H. Stanhope; or "Nothing is so much to be feared as fear," from Thoreau's *Journal*. And the Bible (Proverbs 3:25): "Be not afraid of sudden fear."

* * *

"The ends justify the means," Niccolò Machiavelli's cynical defense for duplicitous conduct. But that is not what he wrote. His original Italian says *"si guarda al fine,"* which means "one must consider the final result." The full thought, in Chapter 18 of his classic *The Prince*, reads, in translation, ". . . .n the actions of all men, and especially of princes, which is not prudent to challenge, one must consider the final result."

* * *

John F. Kennedy is credited with the apothegm, "One man can make a difference and every man should try." But these are the words not of the president, rather of his first lady. Jackie Kennedy had this inscribed on a card that accompanied the traveling exhibit celebrating the opening of the JFK Library in 1979.

* * *

In his first address after becoming Prime Minister in May 1940, Winston Churchill told the House of Commons, "I have nothing to offer but blood, toil, tears, and sweat." Inspirational, but not without antecedents. In 1611 John Donne had written of "teares, or sweat, or blood"; in 1823 Lord Byron had authored "Blood, sweat, and tear-wrung millions"; in 1919 Lord Alfred Douglas informed us that poetry "is forged slowly and patiently, link by link, with sweat and blood and tears."

* * *

Joseph Stalin is supposed to have said, "The death of one man is a tragedy. The death of millions is a statistic." Stalin may have said it, but he didn't originate it. The thought comes from a 1932 essay by German satirist, Kurt Tucholsky, quoting a fictional French diplomat musing about the horrors of war.

* * *

In response to those who took him to task for his unsavory political activities, "Boss" Tweed of Tammany Hall is reported to have said, "As long as I count the votes, what are you going to do about it?" Tweed denied having said any such, which was true. The words were put into his mouth by editorial cartoonist Thomas Nast, who frequency criticized Tweed in *Harper's Weekly*.

* * *

If it's not from Shakespeare, then it must be in the Bible. Such was the prevailing belief, for a long time, about memorable phrases. But memories are all too often fallible, and even if the passage was from the Bible it was frequently misquoted. For example, "Money is the root of all evil." (Not quite the words from scripture. In 1 Timothy 6:10 we find, "For the love of money is the root of all evil."); "Pride goeth before a fall." (The actual verse, in Proverbs 16:18, reads, "Pride goeth before destruction, a haughty spirit before a fall."); "The eye is the window to the soul." (Nope! See Matthew 6:22, "The eye is the lamp of the body; so then if your eye is clear, you whole body will be full of light."); "All things work together for good." (Compare with Romans 8:28, "And we know that in all things God works for the good of those who love him, who have been called according to his purpose."); "Hate the sin, love the sinner." (Actually a loose quote from Gandhi, and similar to St. Augustine: "With love for mankind and hatred of sins."); "God moves in mysterious way." (The nearest Biblical text is in Isaiah 55:8: "For my thoughts are not your thoughts, nether are your ways my ways."); "A fool and his money are soon parted." (An old English proverb attributed to Thomas Tusser in his 1573 "Five Hundred Points of Good Husbandrie."); and "Neither a borrower or a lender be . . . " (This *is* Shakespeare, *Hamlet*, Act I, Scene 3, wherein Polonius advises his son Laertes.)

* * *

Herbert Hoover is believed to have called prohibition "a noble experiment." Actually, what he said was: Prohibition was "a great social and economic experiment, noble in motive."

* * *

George Washington is supposed to have disparaged "entangling alliances" in his Farewell Address. But he didn't quite say that. He did warn against both "passionate attachments" and "inveterate antipathies" to certain foreign countries. It was Thomas Jefferson, in his first inaugural, who committed to "Peace, commerce, and honest friendship with all nations, entangling alliances with none."

* * *

Sam Goldwyn, noted language mutilator, is credited with telling a theatre manager, "When I see the pictures you play in that theatre it makes my hair stand on the edge of my seat." Very Goldwynesque, but this displeasure was voiced not by Goldwyn but by Hungarian director Michael Curtiz, also a known mutilator of the English language.

* * *

Another, attributed to Goldwyn but from the lips of Curtiz, when a stage hand brought back the wrong prop: "The next time I send a damn fool for something, I'll go myself."

* * *

Mae West, the 1930s image of the sexy woman, came to fame with her breathy invitation, "Why don't you come up and see me some time?" Close, but not a bull's-eye; what she really said, to Cary Grant in the movie *She Done Him Wrong*, was, "Why don't you come up some time and see me?"

* * *

And, speaking of Cary Grant, his many mimickers might be surprised to note that in no movie did he ever say, "Judy, Judy, Judy."

* * *

"I don't think we're in Kansas anymore, Toto." Such is what Dorothy, in the movie *The Wizard of Oz*, tells her dog after the cyclone deposits her house in a foreign place. At least that's what we remember. But our memories are a bit off. The message is right, but not quite the words. What she says is, "Toto, I've a feeling we're not in Kansas anymore."

* * *

Nor did James Cagney, in any of his tough-guy roles, address anyone as, "You dirty rat!" The nearest he ever got was in the 1932 film *Taxi*, when he finds a competitor in his girl's closet he takes out his gun and addresses the locked closet door, "Come and out take it, you dirty yellow-bellied rat."

* * *

In the film *Snow White*, the Wicked Witch doesn't say, "Mirror, mirror on the wall. Who's the fairest one of all?" Rather, she asks, "Magic mirror on the wall. Who's the fairest one of all?" And Oliver Twist doesn't beg, "Please, sir, can I have some more?" Rather, his entreaty is, "Please, sir, I want some more."

* * *

In *The Merchant of Venice*, we are not cautioned that "All that glitters is not gold." The original text reads, "All that glisters is not gold." ("Glister" being an early form of the modern "glitter.")

* * *

From an opposite perspective, Gordon Gekko, the rapacious financier in the film *Wall Street*, extols greed as a societal virtue. But he does not say, "Greed is good." Rather, he lectures, "The point is, ladies and gentlemen, that greed, for lack of a better word, is good. Greed is right. Greed works."

* * *

In the movie *Field of Dreams* the anticipation is not "If you build it, they will come." More properly, it is "If you build it, he will come."

* * *

In the film *The Treasure of Sierra Madre*, when the Mexican bandits claim they are state police, Fred C. Dobbs (Humphrey Bogart) asks to see their badges. The response we remember, "We don't need no stinking badges," is not quite what is said. More accurately, he is told, "Badges? We ain't got no badges. I don't have to show you no stinkin' badges!"

* * *

And Captain Kirk of *Star Trek* never implores, "Beam me up, Scotty." What he says is, "Beam me aboard."

* * *

On *Dragnet*, the legendary TV detective drama, Sgt. Friday (Jack Webb) never says, "Just the facts, ma'am." His iconic line is,

"All we want are the facts, ma'am." But the quote did surface in the 1987 film parody with Dan Ackroyd as Sgt. Friday.

* * *

Even the best known quotes may fall prey to doubtful attribution. Carl Sandburg, recipient of the Pulitzer Prize for his multivolume biography of Abraham Lincoln, credited Lincoln as the author of the well-known epigram, "You can fool all of the people some of the time, and some of the people all of the time, but you cannot fool all of the people all of the time." However, when Lincoln's two secretaries published his collected papers and speeches, they doubted that he had said it. Nor could they find it in the text of the speech, which supposedly contained the passage, as it was printed in the local newspaper the day after he spoke in Clinton, Illinois. Rather, *Hoyt's New Cyclopedia of Practical Quotations* identifies showman P. T. Barnum as the source of the quotation. At this late date no one is certain of the author.

SECTION THREE:
EXPERTS AND NAYSAYERS

Nor are the experts to be believed. We expect them to provide final authority, to be able to distinguish the good from the bad, the genuine from the counterfeit, the real from the fanciful. But why are they so often mistaken? They've had years of higher education, years of experience with the relevant issues, years of contact with leaders in their field. And yet they too frequently give us bad information. If they're not lying, they certainly are misleading us. In either case, their reliability is not be taken for granted. Here are a few examples of the experts' lapse of expertise.

"There is not the slightest indication that nuclear energy will ever be obtainable. It would mean that the atom would have to shattered at will."

—Albert Einstein

* * *

"The advancement of the arts from year to year . . . seems to presage the arrival of that period when further improvements must end."
—Harry L. Ellsworth, US Commissioner of Patents, 1844

* * *

"The idea that cavalry will be replaced by these iron coaches is absurd. It is little short of treasonous."
—Aide de Camp to Field Marshall Haig
at the demonstration of tanks, 1916

* * *

"There will never be a bigger plane built." An engineer with Boeing, after the first flight of the 247, a twin-engine plane capable of carrying ten people

* * *

"A rocket will never be able to leave the Earth's atmosphere."
—*The New York Times*, 1936

* * *

"The Panama Canal is actually a thing of the past, and Nature in her works will soon obliterate all traces of French energy and money expended on the isthmus."
—*Scientific American*, January 1941

* * *

"There is practically no chance communications space satellites will be used to provide better telephone, telegraph, television, or radio service inside the United States."

—T. A. M. Craven, FCC Commissioner, 1961

* * *

"Professor Goddard does not know the relation between action and reaction and the need to have something better than a vacuum against which to react. He seems to lack the basic knowledge ladled out daily in high schools."

—1921 a *New York Times* editorial on Robert Goddard's visionary work with rockets

* * *

"The Americans have need of the telephone, but we do not. We have plenty of messenger boys."

—Sir William Preece, Chief Engineer, British Post Office, 1878

* * *

"The cinema is little more than a fad. It's canned drama. What audiences want to see is flesh and blood on the stage."

—Charles Chaplin in 1916, after two years of movie making

* * *

"Space travel is utter bilge."

—Dr. Richard van der Riet Woodley, Astronomer Royal, 1956

* * *

"With regard to the electric light, much has been said for and against it, but I think I may say without fear of contradiction that when the Paris Exhibition closes, electric light will close with it. And no more will be heard of it."

—Erasmus Wilson, Professor, Oxford University, 1878

* * *

"The actual building of roads devoted to motor cars is not for the near future, in spite of many rumors to that effect."

—*Harper's Weekly*, August 2, 1902

* * *

"We can close the books on infectious disease."

—William H. Stewart,
US Surgeon General, addressing Congress in 1969

* * *

"There cannot always be fresh fields of conquest by the knife, there must be portions of the human frame that will ever remain sacred from its intrusions, at least in the surgeon's hand. That we have already, if not quite, reached these final limits, there can be little question. The abdomen, the chest, and the brain, will be forever shut from the intrusion of the wise and humane surgeon."

—Sir John Erichson, President,
Royal College of Surgeons of England, 1873

* * *

"The popular mind often pictures gigantic flying machines speeding across the Atlantic and carrying innumerable passengers in a way analogous to our modern steamships . . . It seems safe to say that such ideas must be wholly visionary . . . "

—Astronomer William H. Pickering,
after the invention of the airplane, Oxford University, 1908

* * *

"The coming of the wireless era will make war impossible, because it will make war ridiculous."

—Guglielo Marconi, 1912

* * *

"There are . . . absolutely no facts either in the records of geology, or in the history of the past, or in the experience of the present, that can be referred to as proving evolution, or the development of one species from another by selection of any kind whatever."

—William Penman Lyon, Congregational minister, 1871

* * *

"My personal desire would be to prohibit entirely the use of alternating currents. They are as unnecessary as they are dangerous."

—Thomas A. Edison, 1889

* * *

"Stocks have reached what looks like a permanently high plateau."

—American economist Irving Fisher,
three days before the market crash, 1929

* * *

"640K ought to be enough for anybody."

—Bill Gates, 1981

* * *

"There are defects about the electric light which, unless some essential change takes place, must entirely prevent its application to ordinary lighting purposes."

—Report from the Select Committee on Lighting by Electricity, House of Commons, 1879

* * *

"Children just aren't interested in witches and wizards anymore."

—Publisher's letter to J. K. Rowling, responding to her proposal for *Harry Potter and the Philosopher's Stone*, 1996

* * *

"As far as sinking a ship with a bomb is concerned, you just can't do it."

—US Rear Admiral Clark Woodward, 1939

* * *

"It'll be gone by June."

—*Variety* magazine's assessment of the future of rock and roll, 1955

* * *

"Has there ever been danger of war between Germany and ourselves, members of the same Teutonic race? Never has it even been imagined."

—Industrialist Andrew Carnegie, 1913

* * *

"Airplanes are interesting toys, but of no military value."
—French Marshall Ferdinand Foch in 1911, later Allied supreme
commander during the final year of the First World War

* * *

"While theoretically and technically television may be feasible, commercially it is an impossibility."
—Lee de Forest, American inventor, "father of radio"

* * *

"X-rays will prove to be a hoax."
—Lord Kelvin, President, the Royal Society, 1883

* * *

"Flight by machines heavier than air is impractical and insignificant, if not utterly impossible."
—Simon Newcomb, astronomer, 1902

* * *

About online shopping: "Remote shopping, while entirely feasible, will flop."
—*Time* magazine, May 1966

* * *

"There's no chance that the iPhone is going to get any significant market share."
—Steve Ballmer, Microsoft CEO, 2007

* * *

"Rail travel at high speed is not possible because passengers, unable to breathe, would die of asphyxia."
—Dionysus Lardner, Professor of Natural Philosophy, University College, London, 1830

* * *

"Everything that can be invented has been invented."
—Charles H. Duell, US Commissioner of Patents, 1899

SECTION FOUR:
POLITICIANS

How can one plan a book about lying without including politicians? Think of the conundrum: How can you tell when a politician is lying? And the answer is, of course, when his lips are moving. It was Will Rogers who observed, "Everything is changing. People are taking their comedians seriously and the politicians as a joke." Politicians have always lied, but recently the quality of their lying has changed. In the past, their falsifications had a kernel of truth, bending the facts a bit to support a favorable conclusion, more misrepresentation than outright invention. Now, "facts" are made up out of thin air, totally devoid of any reality. Observers have labeled this an era of "post-truth politics," in which candidates appeal to voters' feelings, pretty well ignoring facts. Candidates can say anything they want, and they often do. It was Adolf Hitler who proposed, in *Mein Kampf*, that "The great masses of the people will more easily fall victims to a great lie than to a small one." But when listening to political blather, a problem soon arises. How to distinguish between the politician who is lying and the one who is just being stupid. Or being stupid about lying, or lying about being stupid. Things said in the political arena, both falsified and vacuous, are enough to fill several volumes, which I'm sure they have. Here are some quotes providing evidence for Rogers's assertion, a small selection of remarks and/or pronouncements and/or opinions, some newly minted and some classic historical quotes.

The stage is set by Parson Weems with his story of George Washington and the cherry tree, wherein George is quoted as saying, "I cannot tell a lie." Which in itself is a lie, Weems having made it all up. Besides, how can someone with a straight face say he cannot tell a lie? Such a statement demands disbelief. As do many that follow, more choice examples of the cupidity, stupidity or downright lying by the people we elect to govern us.

* * *

Mark Twain is credited with the observation, "We have the best Congress money can buy." In the current political arena the second half of that declaration seems closer to the truth than the first half. The image of politicians has never been so poor, deservedly so. It seems every few months a lead newspaper article concerns some congressman or governor forced to retire because of a financial or sexual indiscretion, either selling influence, lying about covert income or sleeping with a colleague's wife or office assistant.

* * *

Displaying a rare bit of insight, Ronald Reagan once observed, "'Politics is supposed to be the second-oldest profession. I have come to realize that it bears a very close resemblance to the first."

* * *

"We had no domestic attacks under Bush," said Republican apologist Rudy Giuliani, in 2010. "We've had one under Obama." Guiliani apparently forgot (or chose to forget) the 9/11 attack on New York's World Trade Center in 2001, while he was mayor of the city and Bush was president.

* * *

"I did not have sex with that woman," insisted President Clinton at his impeachment hearing in 1998, applying his own definition of sexual activity, debating the meaning of the word "is," and denying what everybody knew to be true.

* * *

Displaying the perceptive intelligence typical of some of our government officials, Donald Rumsfeld, George Bush's Defense Secretary definitively reported in 2003, "We know of certain knowledge that he [Osama Bin Laden] is either in Afghanistan, or in some other country, or dead." And that's for sure!

* * *

Florida judge Harold Carswell made his opinion known in 1948: "Segregation of the races is proper and the only practical and correct way of life in our states." That statement kept Carswell from Senate approval when he was named for the Supreme Court in 1969.

* * *

In a discussion about fiscal policy, Sen. Everett Dirkson mused, "A billion here, a billion there, and pretty soon you're talking about real money."

* * *

White House spokesman Marlin Fitzwater explained the constancy of the Bush administration's national security policy in 1990: "This strategy represents our policy for all time. Until it's changed.

* * *

Intending to make a point in defense of his argument, in 1979 presidential candidate Ronald Reagan cited a nonexistent study supposedly by the EPA which, he said, "reveals that 80 percent of air pollution comes not from chimneys and auto exhaust pipes, but from plants and trees." We still don't know if Eureka College failed to educate him or he was just trying to snow his adversary.

* * *

A confession: "The present system may be flawed, but that's not to say that we in Congress can't make it worse." Said by Representative E. Clay Shaw (R-FL) in 1994, during the debate on health-care reform.

* * *

Sen. Everett Dirkson, Republican Senator from Illinois, once explained his modus operandi: "I am a man of fixed and unbending principles, the first of which is to be flexible at all times."

* * *

A perceptive observation from President Calvin Coolidge: "When many people are out of work, unemployment results."

* * *

Cool Cal allegedly once made a disclosure to actress Ethyl Barrymore: "I think the American public wants a solemn ass as President and I think I'll go along with that." I'll leave it to the reader's opinion whether or not he fulfilled that pledge.

* * *

"Sensible and responsible women do not want to vote." So said ex-President Grover Cleveland in 1905. Maybe not the "sensible and responsible" women he knew. But women did finally get the vote with the ratification of the Nineteenth Constitutional Amendment in 1920.

* * *

In 1988 Sen. Orrin Hatch, Republican from Utah, supporting legislation that would apply the death penalty for drug convictions, justified his resolution with this bit of Kafka-esque logic: "Capital punishment is our society's recognition of the sanctity of human life." And what about triple fines for pleading poverty?

* * *

"Death has a tendency to encourage a depressing view of war." So said Donald Rumsfeld, Defense Secretary under Pres. G. W. Bush, 2003, adding a downer to what would otherwise be a joyful remembrance.

* * *

Presidential candidates also suffer memory lapses, as witness this trace from Barack Obama, at a campaign stop in Oregon in May 2008: "I've now been in fifty-seven states, I think one left to go."

* * *

"An honest politician is one who, when he's bought stays bought." So said Simon Cameron, President Lincoln's Secretary of War.

* * *

Dismayed by events, President Gerald Ford once voiced this astute observation: "If Lincoln were alive today, he'd roll over in his grave." On a different occasion, Ford also perceived that, "Things are more like they are now than they have ever been."

* * *

Reflecting on his loss in his run for New Jersey's governorship in 1957, magazine publisher Malcolm Forbes lamented, "We were nosed out by a landslide." His son Steve repeated the same observation when he pulled out of the 2000 presidential race.

* * *

"Democracy used to be a good thing, but it has now got into the wrong hands." A lamentation by ultraconservative Sen. Jesse Helms of North Carolina.

* * *

"Gaiety is the outstanding feature of the Soviet Union."
—Joseph Stalin in 1935

* * *

"The Middle East is obviously an issue that has plagued the region for centuries."
—President Obama, musing about one the world's impenetrables

* * *

The most consistent contributors to our survey of absurdity seems to be Republican vice presidents or VP candidates. Democrats can of course be equivalently nonsensical, just not as often. Consider these selections from Dan Quayle, VP to G. H. W. Bush: "I love California, I practically grew up in Phoenix." Or, "I understand the importance of bondage between parent and child." Or, "It isn't pollution that's harming the environment. It's the impurities in our air and water that are doing it." Or, "It's wonderful to be here in the great state of Chicago." Or, "This President is going to lead us out of this recovery." Or, "The global importance of the Middle East is that it keeps the Far East and the Near East from encroaching on each other." Or, "One word sums up probably the responsibility of any vice president, and that one word is 'to be prepared'." Or, "I was recently on a tour of Latin America, and the only regret I have was that I didn't study Latin harder in school so I could converse with those people." Or, "Verbosity leads to unclear, inarticulate things." Or, "We are ready for any unforeseen event that may or may not occur." Or, summing up in 1989, "I stand by all the misstatements that I've made."

* * *

Or these, from the "woefully ignorant" Sarah Palin (so designated by one of her ex-staffers), presidential candidate Jon McCain's VP running mate in 2008: "But obviously, we've got to stand with our North Korean allies," when interviewed by Glenn Beck, November 23, 2010. Or, "There's no convincing scientific evidence for man-made climate change. The climate has always been changing." Or, "Waterboarding is how we baptize terrorists." Or, "[Barack and Michelle Obama] have power in their words. They could refudiate [sic!] what it is that this group is saying." Or, "I think on a national level your Department of Law there in the White House would look at some of the things that we've been charged with and automatically throw them out." (Note: There is no Department of Law.) Or, ". . . .round this great northwest—here in New Hampshire you just get it." Or, ". . . .here is hope and opportunity in our neighboring country of Afghanistan." Or, "We North Americans, we come from the stock of our ancestors." Or, "If God had not intended us to eat animals, how come he made them out of meat?"

* * *

"I think gay marriage is something that should be between a man and a woman."

—California's ex-governor, Arnold Schwarzenegger

* * *

"You know what, evolution is a myth. Why aren't monkeys still evolving into humans?'"

—Christine O'Donnell, later Tea Party candidate for the US Senate from Delaware, during a 1998 appearance on Bill Maher's *Politically Incorrect*.

* * *

Describing their administration's commitment to equality, Reagan's interior secretary James Watt described an advisory group thus, "We have every kind of mixture you can have. I have a black, I have a woman, two Jews, and a cripple." Watt later resigned.

* * *

California's Representative Barbara Boxer (D-CA) reacting to a local earthquake: "Those who survived the San Francisco earthquake said 'Thank God, I'm still alive.' But, of course, those who died, their lives will never be the same again."

* * *

The second President Bush felt it necessary to establish his autonomy from his advisors: "I have opinions of my own, strong opinions. But I don't always agree with them."

* * *

In defense of sexual equality, Claire Sargent, 1992 Arizona senatorial candidate, suggested: "I think it's about time we voted for senators with breasts. After all, we've been voting for boobs long enough."

* * *

"The depression is over."

—Herbert Hoover, June 1930

* * *

John Wilkes, British PM, was charged by the Earl of Sandwich: "I do not know whether you will die upon the gallows or of the pox." Wilkes responded, "That must depend, milord, upon whether I first embrace your lordship's principles or your lordship's mistresses."

* * *

Winston Churchill was confronted by a woman who complained he was drunk. "Yes, I am," he responded. "And you're ugly. But tomorrow I'll be sober."

* * *

"That's the most unheard-of thing I ever heard of."

—Wisconsin's Sen. Joseph McCarthy responding to a witness's testimony during the infamous "witch-hunt" investigation into so-called communist infiltration in the US government in the 1950s

* * *

"I think the free-enterprise system is absolutely too important to be left to the voluntary action of the marketplace."
—Representative Richard Kelly (D-FL), who was later convicted
for taking bribes in the 1970 Abscam scandal.

* * *

When asked about the potential use of missiles in the Persian Gulf War in 1991, Defense Dept. spokesman Pete Williams told reporters, "We don't discuss that capability. I can't tell you why we don't discuss it because then I'd be discussing it."

* * *

You think your Congress is the worst ever? Know that the forty-second Congress of 1873 gave itself a 50 percent salary increase, then proceeded to make it retroactive for two years, to the beginning of its term.

* * *

Which brings us to the 2016 presidential election and our 45th president, Donald Trump, the novice who beat out sixteen other candidates in the Republican primary and won the general election with 306 electoral votes to Hillary Clinton's 232, although Clinton amassed three million more popular votes than he did. But in typical Trump fashion he first ignored reality and claimed that his popular vote was bigger than hers, then later attributed her plurality to voting by "illegal aliens."

Trump's campaign was characterized by his playing loose with facts. During the primary the *News York Times* noted that "Routine falsehoods, unfounded claims and inflammatory language have long been staples of Mr. Trump's campaign." Another commentator labeled him "a serial fabricator."

Here are a few of his campaign pronouncements:

Brandishing his huge knowledge of international affairs: "I know Russia well, I had a major event there two or three years ago—Miss Universe contest."

Or, on *60 Minutes*, immodestly boasting of his modesty: "I think I'm more humble than you would understand."

Or, in his anti-Mexican mode, "When Mexico sends its people, they're not sending their best. They're sending people with lots of problems. They're bringing drugs. They're bringing crime. They're rapists." And elsewhere: "I will build a great, great wall on our southern border and I will make Mexico pay for that wall. Mark my words."

Or, displaying his disdain for Muslims by distorting the news when interviewed on *Meet the Press* about the 9/11 destruction of the World Trade Center: "I watched in Jersey City, New Jersey, when thousands and thousands of people were cheering as that building was coming down." (When asked for a reaction, a supporter said, simply. "He's exaggerating.")

Or, after the Brexit vote: "Just arrived in Scotland. Place is going wild over the vote. They took their country back, just like we will take America back." (Apparently unable to distinguish between Scotland and the UK, he seems unaware that Scotland voted to stay in the EU.)

Or simply making things up: "I'll never forget the scene this morning . . . of taking that money off that airplane." (Here he was reporting viewing a top secret tape of an American plane unloading cash in Iran as payment for something undefined, possibly as ransom for the release of four Americans. His campaign acknowledged that no such footage exists.)

Or accusing the chairwoman of the Federal Reserve of corruption, or President Obama of being "the founder" of ISIS, or Hillary Clinton of starting the birther movement, or charging conspiracy any time he came off looking foolish or uninformed. Either the debate moderator was biased, or the crowd was antagonistic, or his microphone was defective, or some other diversion to avert responsibility for his own shortcomings. All the while repeatedly labeling any uncomplimentary reporting as "false news."

Trump's campaign had become so obviously fanciful that *POLITICO* magazine felt it necessary to do a wide-ranging fact-check of just one random week of his public utterances. The final report: ". . . .ore than five dozen statements deemed mischaracter-izations, exaggerations, or simply false. . . .t equates to roughly one misstatement every five minutes on average."

A political news registry, monitoring his performance after being sworn in, recorded sixteen substantive untruths in the first month of his presidency. Though literally dozens of his statements have been debunked, no one has been able to determine whether he was intentionally mouthing falsehoods or was simply unable to distinguish truth from fantasy.

But his impotence in truth-telling soon became characteristic of his administration. Trump's blatant disregard for reality early on infected his new staff. Within a few days of taking office, during his first formal meeting with the press corps, Sean Spicer, Trump's press spokesman, was caught in four or five obvious untruths. In defense of Spicer's fabrications, Trump's erstwhile campaign manager and now White House advisor, Kellyanne Conway, said Spicer was merely stating "alternative facts," thereby creating a new concept of political lying. Several commentators found the mindset redolent of George Orwell's *1984*.

As this is being written, Mr. Trump having fired the head of the FBI who had opened an investigation into some of his campaign's suspicious activities, a special prosecutor has been appointed to look into his campaign's possible collusion with Russia. Most of his supporters are downplaying the potential consequences of this investigation, though some have already run for the hills, while his detractors are hoping for his impeach-ment.

* * *

Attempting to balance the scales, I offer a few voices in rebuttal: "Under democracy one party always devotes its chief energies to trying to prove that the other party is unfit to rule and both commonly succeed, and are right."

—H. L. Mencken

* * *

"The problem with political jokes is they get elected."

—Henry Cate VII

* * *

And an astute observation by José Maria de Eça de Queiroz, the great Portuguese writer: "Politicians and diapers should be changed frequently and all for the same reason."

* * *

In closing, we note that the United States Constitution, the remarkable instrument upon which our nation is built, starts out with an egregious grammatical error. The prefatory statement begins, "We the People of the United States, in Order to form a more perfect Union. . ." But "more perfect" is conspicuously bad English. Perfect is not subject to gradations, it is an all-or-nothing concept; either a thing is perfect or it's not. So, while we glory in the magnificence of our founding document, we can still wish it had been conceived with more perfect grammar.